TRUST
FOR
TODAY

365 DAYS OF
ENCOURAGEMENT

A YEAR WITH THE **TRUEFACE** TEAM

THE CURE
Our foundational book on why our primary motive is to trust God.

THE CURE AND PARENTS
Written in short episodes applying grace to family.

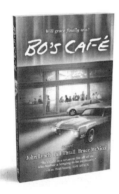

BO'S CAFE
A novelization of grace in marriage and trusting others.

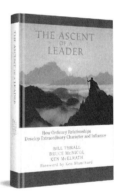

THE ASCENT OF A LEADER
Create environments of trust as a leader.

 **@TRUEFACELIFE**

GRAB YOUR PHONE AND FOLLOW US ON INSTAGRAM FOR NEW APPLICATIONS IN GRACE EACH WEEK.

HEART OF MAN MOVIE & GUIDE
What if sexual brokenness wasn't a barrier but a bridge?
Watch this powerful film.

BEHIND THE MASK
Succinctly addresses how grace interacts with sin.
eBook only.

ON MY WORST DAY
A humorous autobiographical walk through trying to live life in grace.

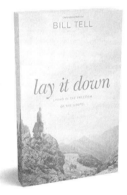

LAY IT DOWN
A biblical exploration of grace from our associate Bill Tell.

TABLE OF CONTENTS

TRUEFACE

For over 20 years the team at Trueface has been writing, speaking, consulting and dreaming about how to help leaders trust God and others with them. We are still doing that while we passionately grow the diversity of voices who are bringing this freedom to the world. With strong contributions from nearly a dozen men and women across three generations, this effort brings daily encouragement and application from the growing unity in diversity that grace can foster. To see more about the team on this book go to www.trueface.org We want to encourage you with our books, courses and speaking.

You can join us in getting this message out. If you believe this book will encourage people, please say so on Amazon reviews. If you would like to give the book to friends get bulk discounts at trueface.store.You can also start sharing our quick encouragements from Instagram and Facebook. Follow us here: Instagram: @TruefaceLife, Facebook: facebook.com/truefacecommunity.

Trueface is a non-profit that works very hard to sustain through excellent services and products. We aim for a strong 50/50 model that pairs with your investments in this work. We would deeply appreciate your support and will continue our transparent practices held to that excellence by our ECFA membership for non-profit financial governance.

INTRODUCTION

Welcome, friend!

For a long time, our team at Trueface has wanted to offer a devotional. In some ways a daily devotional may be the best vehicle to show how grace, trust, love and identity in Christ work themselves out in everyday life—in ordinary and extraordinary moments, in complex relationships, in your talks and thoughts with God, or when someone cuts you off in traffic and gestures obscenely as they speed away. We want to explore our deepest longings and face some of the hard questions of scripture. We want this book to encompass the pain, the loss, the success, and the grief. It's difficult to believe that Jesus has really made us new creatures with a new identity, and learning to live out of that starts in the day-to-day. We want it to be sacred, honest, playful and funny—just like our lives.

We hope you find yourself on every page. We hope you'll read it this year and maybe every year. We hope you'll invite others to experience it with you.

"When we swim in the ocean of God's grace we can't help but respond with playful abandon."

-TrueFaced (now The Cure)

J A N U A R Y

 @truefacecommunity | @truefacelife

HI

Dear Reader,

It's me, God. Before this world began, this moment with you was planned—by Me, God. I saw it and created it. Everything. That is unless you're sitting in a motel. I lay no claim to that fake oil painting and its frame.

Anyway, here we are. Eternity comes into real time in a page from a devotional book. I am now inhabiting this moment as you are reading these words. I am right here—Me, God.

And so before you go do what you do, I want you to know this: I am delighted with you. I am fully invested in and working in your life every single moment. I've been up ahead and I see what we will get to do and who you will mature into. And I am smiling. That's all. I just wanted you to know. I love you.

Sincerely, God

Isaiah 46:10

ALREADY CHANGED

Are you someone who might someday change into who you're supposed to be? Or are you a newly created being the second you trust in Jesus, who gets to mature into who you already are?

Your answer will largely determine whether you live in vibrant freedom or rarely content striving.

The Christian life is not about changing into someone different but about living out of who you already are.

Paul says, in 2 Corinthians 5:17, "If anyone is in Christ, he is a new creature; the old things passed away; behold new things have come."

Paul doesn't say, "He's saved, but he's still an old chunk of coal—maybe a diamond someday. Maybe."

God's very nature indwells you. You still carry the ability to sin. But the essence of your being has been rewired.

What difference would it make to believe you're already a diamond? You might stop faking or putting on appearances. You might stop trying to be good enough, believing that you already are.

You might rest in what God's already done in you.

Romans 8:9

JUST AS YOU ARE

Some of us discover as we grow older that we are inordinately affected by others' perceptions of us. It can haunt us and leave us feeling insecure.

The gospel's got some great news for such as us. The more we risk believing how well we are loved, the more comfortable we become in our own skin.

"Wouldn't He have better loved a 'me' version without my weaknesses, flaws, and disfigured toes?"

Apparently not. He saw it all and still intentionally brought you here. You. Exactly you. Isn't that mind-blowing? There is not one person on this planet He loves more.

Also, believing your lovability will make you more attractive to others. You'll display an infectious joy in knowing you are fully known and enjoyed by the One who matters most in the galaxy.

This may take awhile to mature into. Relax. He cares more about you getting these truths than you do.

In the meantime, stripes make you look wider and black makes you look thinner (or is it the other way around?).

Psalm 139:1-6

AN OTHERWISE LAW-ABIDING CITIZEN

He cut you off in traffic. Then, to rub it in, he flipped you off. And you didn't do anything wrong!

You're an otherwise law-abiding citizen. But suddenly, without any thought of repercussion, your first response is to pull up alongside his car, roll down your window, and throw the remainder of your hamburger value meal at his El Camino.

Here's some help. The indignation you're feeling is legitimate. But you get to be above this, largely because you know how much you're worth to God. Most people spend their lives trying to blow up the balloon of self-worth. A rude driver can pop that in a flash. The issue of your worth has already been settled. So instead, take a deep breath, smile, and let it go. You've got immensely bigger fish to fry than chasing an unhealthy El Camino. Just say to yourself, "He's probably late to his anger-management class." Enjoy your value meal. It's too good a deal to waste on a car window.

Colossians 3:12-17

NEW

Throughout these devotions you'll read the believer described as "new," with a new spiritual DNA. This needs some defining or it can drift into religious jargon, never touching the reality of your life.

"New" describes what happened the moment you put your hope and trust in Jesus. You didn't just get a ticket to heaven but an entirely new identity! You couldn't see it if a surgeon opened you up, but a supernatural exchange took place.

Christ in you. No longer God only in heaven.

Acts 2 describes when the Trinity first took up residence in believers—Father, Son, and Holy Spirit able at once to be in heaven and in you. (And you thought explaining the virgin birth was tricky.)

God's righteousness imparted into you. *Actually*. Not metaphorically. You may not be mature in it, but it's still true.

No longer just the old you down here slogging it out.

You are fully righteous.

2 Corinthians 5:21

LETTING THE LIGHT SHINE THROUGH

A group of friends traveling through Europe were surprised by a stretch of neighborhood in the Netherlands. It was almost dusk. But every home had lights on inside and appeared to have no curtains. You could see through their entire home! What would cause families to do this?

A local explained, "During the war, they were forced to shut their drapes and turn off lights, to avoid becoming targets of the Luftwaffe. They lived that way, in fear and hiding. It was a way of life. You stayed quiet and let no one see you. One day, at war's end, they agreed to never live that way again. Now it's hard to locate a drape shop in the entire country!"

What a beautiful picture of our redeemed lives in Christ! Many of us held up for years, draped behind fear and shame. How bravely alive to say, "No more. I will live open, true, and free. There may be danger, but I will not live my life unknown. No more drapes."

1 John 1:5-10

JESUS AND THE TRUTH

Dostoevsky's creed:

"I believe there is nothing lovelier, deeper, more sympathetic and more perfect than the Savior; I say to myself with jealous love that not only is there no one else like Him, but that there could be no one. I would say even more. If any one could prove to me that Christ is outside the truth, and if the truth really did exclude Christ, I should prefer to stay with Christ and not with the truth."

It is, in one sense, nonsense. For Jesus would not be the One we adore if He wasn't completely in line with truth. He created truth. The truth will never exclude Christ. We will never need to choose between the two. But if it somehow came down to it, and we did have to make such a choice, we would only stand closer to Jesus. For we know that in His good time, He'd make sense of all that seemed to us destructive and vilifying.

Stay with Christ. And all will be well.

John 1:14

THE FLESH

So how can you be an entirely new creature and still struggle with sin, temptation, and self-deception?

It can break your heart to fall in love with Jesus only to discover you still have the capacity to fail Him in almost every manner possible.

Nothing befuddled the apostle Paul more. He spent Romans 5–8 talking about this.

He calls it "the flesh." It can still sin.

But it's not the real you. The flesh is really no match for the Spirit in you, but when you try to fight it yourself, it beats you up. It is unredeemable and cannot be solved by willpower.

Every believer carries this dynamic.

The flesh works best in darkness, hiding, and self-protectiveness.

So your best protection against the flesh is humility, trust, love, and being loved.

When you believe you are a new creation with a shame-free identity, the flesh has little base to operate from.

You need not dwell on the flesh. It's subdued by three words: "Christ in me."

Romans 7:18

LIVING WITH IMPERFECTIONS

Some neighborhoods are quiet, with the aroma of orange blossoms. Others border freeways, and on warm days smell like cat urine.

It's easy to romanticize the former and dismiss the latter.

Yet some of the most miserable people live in the former while some of the most genuinely happy live in the latter.

It's a classic case of *contentment*—defined as "the ability to see God's goodness independent of the quality of the sights, sounds, and smells."

Live somewhere long enough and you'll start to notice imperfections. It can be even more betraying to discover them where you thought you wouldn't.

Unless you're convinced you're always receiving His best love wherever you find yourself, you can easily let the imperfections drown you. If this happens, then you'll either give in to resignation or begin searching for a new house, or possibly spouse.

Contentment is becoming reconciled to imperfections as you preoccupy yourself with that which is truly perfect—God's love for you and the life He has chosen to love you in.

Now you're living.

Philippians 4:11-13

DAILY QUESTIONS

If love at its very essence is the process of meeting another's needs, then the one who loves gets to ask this question: "What are the needs of the people who trust me?" Many people go through an entire life-time never asking such a question. They go from day to day, only responding to their circumstances. But you can be intentionally pro-active with your capacity to love. You can be a part of changing the trajectory of lives around you by observing their longings, wounds, and weaknesses.

Those who love get to ask another trajectory-changing question: "What are those needs of mine that I'm willing to let others have ac-cess to and love me by meeting?" It feels fragile to ask this. But what a gift you offer a friend when you say, "You are someone I trust with my life. In this particular area, I think you could help me very much. Would you be willing to help meet my need?"

These questions, asked frequently, are the best questions we can ask each other.

Proverbs 12:15

INTEGRITY TO SAY, "I DON'T KNOW"

In our longing to defend God and convince others there are answers to all questions, we can give the appearance that we're know-it-alls. We're not. We offer an immeasurable gift to others when we learn to say, "I don't know the answer to that."

Just because we have the "mind of Christ" does not mean we have all the answers of Christ. Jesus is quite able to defend Himself. If we can represent Him with humility, authenticity, and loving compassion, then we open the door for others to investigate His love.

In admitting we don't know something, we're not telling people there are not answers. They know that. And we're not saying we don't care or are uninterested in their question. What we are saying is, "I will not bluff you. If you'd like, I'll search this out with you. I think I might be as interested in the answer as you are." God smiles at such integrity.

Philippians 2:5-11

WHEN LEADERS REJECT GRACE

Grace can feel especially intimidating to leaders, pastors, and writers who've built successful platforms by teaching their constituents a behavior-management gospel. In such cases, it's appropriately intimidating to consider the possibility that actual righteousness and total acceptance could be true. It could take the wind out of the sails of a church ship that has been moving along nicely, appealing to the flesh to accomplish a "higher walk with God." A pastor or educator may reasonably ask, "Why would I risk leaving my boat dead in the water?"

If you are in such a community, first, continue loving the leader well. Second, invite them to read a thoughtful book or take a biblical course on the gospel of grace—but only if you sense an openness. You don't sell grace; you offer it when the time is right. Sometimes, the time becomes "right" after a leader has failed financially, morally, domestically, or vocationally. Often, they'll be receptive to someone who's been embodying love, grace and trust all along. Someone like you.

Galatians 1:6-7

NO MORE BOOGEYMEN

There will always be preachers and writers who contend believers are best motivated by fear. They'll preach the scriptures partially to inject concern that we should be doing more to make sure we're really saved. We call these the "boogeyman" verses. A boogeyman was that horrifying creature parents used to threaten their kids with if they misbehaved.

Here's an example: Philippians 2:12 says, "work out your salvation with fear and trembling." These teachers thunder this verse to keep us terrified we haven't done enough to "work out" our salvation. It can shake our confidence in grace and our completed identity in Christ. Now, "fear" and "trembling" mean exactly what they seem. The important question to ask is, "What are we to be afraid of?"

The next verse gives us the answer: "for it is God who is at work in you, both to will and to work for His good pleasure" (Philippians 2:13). God's done everything to accomplish your salvation—past, present and future. That should inspire an awe that leaves us trembling and fearful of His power and goodness at work in our lives!

Philippians 2:12-13

BOLDLY, GENTLY

You know a friend is struggling, probably secretly failing at something. You know them well enough to sense something isn't right. But you're not sure how to approach them because they're pretending. Sin can make you self-unaware and a little stupid.

God can use you to bring a friend out of hiding and into the light. The apostle Paul gives a beautiful approach in Galatians 6:1-2. Whether your friend has been caught or may be caught, your approach is similar: "Restore such a one in a spirit of gentleness; each one looking to yourself, so that you too will not be tempted."

You come with *gentleness.* You know you're capable of similar failure. You're being used by God to woo your friend's new heart to tell on themselves. You're attempting to give them a way to come clean, instead of being caught. The route to their restoration could depend upon your approach.

So go boldly, gently.

Galatians 6:1-2

GIVING YOUR TIME AWAY

Even the statement makes it sound like you're losing something. Giving your time *away*. It's true. You cannot retrieve that time. Time is spent. But some time spent is more valuable. Time *taken* in self-entitlement is not of the same blessedness or joyfulness as time given (see Acts 20:35). Both are going to be spent, but time given loving others or in sacrificial action you'll look back on as some of the very best time invested.

The way you spend time can either bless you or rob you of blessing. Let's say you live to 85. You've got somewhere around 744,600 hours to spend. You might spend a quarter of those sleeping and another 150 at the DMV. But the other 558,300 are at your discretion. You were designed to love with much of that time. Sure, some of the hours are to relax, rejuvenate, and read. But the remaining reveals how well you've come to understand love. Giving your time away almost always makes you wonderfully happy. Not a bad use of 300,000-plus hours.

Acts 20:35

TENSION

Some tension is good. Exercise can be described as the body in and out of tension. The creative process employs tension. But there is a tension mixed with shame that is not good. It can create a debilitating anxiety that robs you of your joy.

It wakes you up shouting, "Hey! You're so far behind that you'll never catch up! And just wait because something's coming to ruin you."

What if we could live without this debilitating tension? Grace says we can.

Shame spits, "There is something fundamentally unacceptable with your very person. You'll never be enough. You're nothing but a huge disappointment."

But God whispers, "You are more than enough. I saw today before the world began. I am not embarrassed by you or with you, no matter what happens. You are a joy to me."

Love's voice eases us, helps us un-tense, and allows us to live joyfully in the startling awareness of grace.

Psalm 94:19

CHRIST IN US

Few biblical concepts are at once more plain and yet more difficult to comprehend than Jesus living in a believer. It seems simple enough. God claims to now live in each of us. We're no longer who we were before. We're now "Christ in us." We are humans containing deity—God, who is vitally fused within us. The impossible became possible—the God of the universe, fully in heaven and fully indwelling us.

Many don't seem to believe it. The conflicting terminology is rampant. "I must decrease so that Christ can increase." "My heart cannot be trusted." "If I want something, it must not be what God wants."

No truth will free us more than embracing the power, goodness, and love of "Christ in us." You don't have to understand how it happened, but it is vital to live in the reality of this truth.

Meditate on these verses as though the quality of your life depended upon believing them. Because it does.

Colossians 1:27

TRUSTING VS. PLEASING

At first the title sounds like we're pitting two things against each other that shouldn't be.

But the contrast hints at a very important starting point: How is God pleased?

Either He's pleased with us by what He's already done, or it's up to us to do more to impress Him. Are you doing enough in trusting Him with you, or is there more you must do to be sure?

Was what Jesus did on the cross enough? Or must we keep adding to it to make God happy?

If it's the second, we just have to keep grinding it out, figuring out how many right things we must accumulate and how few wrong things we can get away with. Either we obey Him to make Him pleased with us, or we obey Him because we're convinced He is *already* pleased with us.

Hebrews 11:6 says that what He has done is enough, period. So any effort to please Him through our good works is wasted effort.

He's pleased. Period. Or rather, exclamation point!

Hebrews 11:6

GRACE TO THE HUMBLE

There is only one condition of a person's heart that scripture claims is always guaranteed to receive the grace of God: humility. A good working definition is *trusting God and others with you*.

Humility is the choice to allow another access to you. It is the realization that you simply cannot protect yourself, and so you seek out others who can see you more accurately and assess your life more clearly.

Yes, it's such a scary thing to do. You are the only one you've ever trusted to tinker around with you. But such a humble posture elicits God's grace, which is always sufficient.

Think about the life issues in front of you. Why not try trusting God with the concerns most precious to you? What does God most want you to value in these relationships and life choices? What choices would you make differently? What would it look like?

These are the types of questions trust enjoys asking—humble questions.

1 Peter 5:5

MORE THAN TOLERANCE

Although an immensely popular concept, *tolerance* is one of the great enemies to love. Tolerance carries the idea of begrudgingly putting up with someone who may disagree, oppose, violate, or even disgust us and our sensibilities. Tolerance may be the highest adherence government can require of its citizens. But it does not solve societal enmity. Seething just beneath the veneer of tolerant civility is active hatred waiting to be enflamed by a national, ethnic, or political spark.

Sometimes people who claim they can't tolerate intolerance get confused and display the most intolerance. Tolerance is better than intolerance, no doubt. But the two live in the same neighborhood.

Jesus calls us to blow past tolerance to love even our most dreaded enemies, even when we witness violence, wars, and rumors of war. Love, lived out by Christ-lovers, has the ability to draw all men and women to Himself. We may never see this completely, but it is completely possible. We are the tribe that transcends all nationalism into the very realm of God's kingdom.

Luke 6:27-35

VULNERABILITY VS. TRANSPARENCY

Why is it you can be around someone telling you personal things about themselves and yet you still feel outside their loop? Maybe it's because there's a chasm of difference between *transparency* and *vulnerability.*

Transparency is choosing to disclose yourself to others but in ways you choose. You're being open but you're in control, with little intention of letting anyone in. Preachers have oft been accused of this selective openness.

In vulnerability, you not only tell the truth about you but also allow others in to help. You're giving others permission to know the pain of your weakness, allowing them to care for you. You're not only allowing yourself to come out of hiddenness, but you are also no longer pretending you can solve what you've revealed. The important point is not that something gets fixed, but that nothing ever has to be hidden.

Have you been transparent or vulnerable with the issues in your life? Who would you let in to ask for their care and help?

1 Peter 1:22

SAVED SINNERS OR SAINTS WHO SIN?

If we do what we do because we're trying to be more of something, we will perform to become that "something." If we know we've been made truly righteous by the finished work of Jesus and are loved as His precious children, already completely joined with Christ, well, then we'll gradually learn to live out of who we already are. We will glorify God with our actions instead of trying to assuage shame through performance.

At the center of everything is this question: Are we saved sinners or righteous saints who still sin? Will we claw and fight for something we already have, or will we give away our lives, knowing we are fully righteous and endlessly delighted in and enjoyed, even when nothing seems to be going right? Yes, there are both/and scenarios. But this one's an either/or.

How we answer makes all the difference in the world.

Romans 8:9-11

AFTER THE UGLY WORDS

This is for friends, colleagues, and couples. Or anyone who knows such.

So, about that fight three days ago. It got away from you. You discovered how mean and hurtful you can both be to each other. You've since said the right things and life is going on again. But broken trust and the ugly words you said continue to leave you guarded with each other, totally gun-shy.

Consider this: Maybe this crisis is an invitation into a more authentic, respectful, and kind relationship. It will start with words of humility: "I am so sorry. Please tell me, when you are ready, how my meanness has been affecting you. Our relationship needs an intentionality with Jesus that no longer allows issues to seethe beneath the surface. What amends do I need to make? I am sorry for what I said and did. I want to be forgiven and to honestly forgive you."

This could be the true beginning of the relationship you were hoping to have all along.

Galatians 5:13-26

WINNABLE AUTHORITY

It seems like such an innocuous question: "How am I affecting you?" Why would anyone ask it? But it could change the course of your family. To ask it, you're admitting, "I think I'm affecting my family in good ways but also in some damaging ways. And they're the only ones who can tell me what I'm blind to." Without giving up your authority, you can disarm their fear of being honest.

They start to see you as winnable authority.

At first they may fear there's a catch: "If I answer honestly, I'm going to pay." You must convince them that they won't, and then deliver. They may initially offer up something benign. But on maybe the twentieth ask, you might hear, "Sometimes you scare me. Like you just want me to shut up. So I do."

Don't overreact. Don't defend. Just listen. Say thank you. Then own your wrong. Convince them you believe them by asking them how to change it. That's winning.

Proverbs 25:15

WALKING IN THE LIGHT

Have you heard that phrase before? It sounds a bit religious and raises a few questions: What kind of walking, and how much light? How do you know if you're doing it right? It sounds rather subjective and, frankly, wearying.

But what if it's none of that? Walking in the light is living with nothing hidden. When scripture talks of light, it often contrasts it with the darkness of hiddenness. Ephesians 5:13 says, "But all things become visible when they are *exposed* by the light, for everything that becomes visible *is* light."

Choosing to live with nothing hidden is a choice of the heart. You decide to give up pretending you're someone better than you are. You are trusting that God can handle what is really true about you and He can protect you in whatever is revealed.

The choice is costly. You give up a double life. But you experience the clarity light gives to everything it shines on. You can walk in the light in this moment.

Ephesians 5:13

OUR DEAR GOD

"Our dear God. We come from cities and towns all around the world. Some of us live in blight, others live in opulence. Some of us are shattered, others are astonished at the beauty of our lives. But we all find ourselves shaking our heads in gratitude that You found us. We continued making destructive choices, even after we were found. You refuse to rub our noses into it. No matter what we do or where we go, You refuse to moderate the intensity of Your love. You don't keep records, You don't bring up past stuff. Your love is as present and immediate as our next breath.

Our tendency is to want to pay You back. We want to say, 'What can we do for You?' You will have none of it. You only want a trusting heart.

So we stop right here, in this moment, and rest in trusting You. We love You. And we receive Your love—imperfectly, but You are fine with that."

Jude 1:24-25

MONEY MATTERS

Perhaps, the most important people who will ever learn from your money wisdom are the children and young adults God puts in your path. They most indelibly learn your wisdom when they see your *action*. How you earn, save, invest, spend, and give.

For example, if you live as if "God owns it all," including money, they can absorb gratitude rather than greed. If you believe the amount God entrusts you with is not the important thing, but how you handle that amount, then even children can experience the joy of simple budgeting and giving small amounts.

You may be thinking, "But, I have so much to learn about finances myself." Perfect. Your learner's attitude toward money actually engenders a curiosity in them, rather than fear or denial about finances. Many resources are available to help you. Let one who has helped thousands, Ron Blue, encourage you with his teachability, "God is at work in my life and has used my good and bad decisions with my finances to teach me more about who He is."

Luke 16:11-12

WITHOUT TRUST (PART ONE)

Without trust, I cannot meet God. Without trust, I cannot please God. Without trust, I cannot experience truth and freedom. The truth will not set me free unless I trust it. If I don't trust you, then I can't experience your love, no matter how much love you have for me. Without trust, I can develop competencies, wealth, and power, but at the expense of relationships. Without trust, I cannot cultivate safe communities where the truth can flow.

Trust is not a vague, theoretical nicety. Trust risks allowing another to meet my needs. As I learn to trust in the abilities and care of another, I opt to no longer pretend I can protect myself. Without trust, I am pretending I am self-sufficient. And I am not. Without trust, I cannot be guided into who I am or into the fulfillment of God's purposes for my life.

2 Corinthians 1:9-11

WITHOUT TRUST (PART TWO)

Truth only transforms when it's trusted. Without trust, we live in isolation. We are hidden, immature, and vulnerable to our weaknesses. Without trust, truth is relative. We live as our own expert. Without trust, we live with fear. The love of God will not cast out fear unless we trust that love. Without trust, internal comparisons siphon away energy. Without trust, children live without direction. Without trust, pleasure is substituted for intimacy.

Without trust, power is pursued as the weak are ignored. Without trust, rights are demanded as the basis for fulfillment. Without trust, the shame story we tell ourselves feeds emotional and relational sickness. Without trust, we lose hope. Without trust, we lose our identity. Without trust, we are trapped in a mindset of "I ought to…" Without trust, we can reach our potential but can never experience our destiny.

Luke 18:9-14

WHERE IS GOD IN MY PAIN?

You can face chronic, even inexplicable, physical pain. But what pain tries to tell you about you is often unbearable. Several on our team have faced chronic pain for years, and we realize that pain mixed with shame can sometimes try to convince us that this pain is our fault, that God doesn't really care, and that we are on our own.

Unmasking the lies of pain allows you to endure it in a redeeming, even joyful, way. Jesus endured the cross to overcome the "shame lies" of your pain. God has entered fully and completely into the center of your pain. No theologian can explain how the same God playfully present at a four-year-old's birthday party can also stand in the storm of your chronic, debilitating pain. But it is somehow true.

For those who have put their hope in Him, God somehow causes all things to ultimately work out for good. Yes, this sounds impossible. And it doesn't magically take away the pain. But you can endure. For God cares. And you are never alone.

Philippians 3:10

WHO I ALREADY AM

Consider this statement: The Christian life is not about changing into someone else but about living out of who I already am.

What would that change in the way I interact with God? Well, I might stop hiding, afraid He thinks I haven't changed enough. I might not work so frantically to be accepted but instead enjoy my acceptance. I might sin less, convinced that choosing that sin is not coming from the real me. I might love more instead of trying to sin less.

I might begin to feel comfortable in my own skin. I might not have to put on a mask for others, afraid they can see through to the insufficiently changed me. I might let God love me instead of fearing His judgment. I might simply love Him instead of performing for His love.

Consider how incredible that would feel.

Ephesians 1:5-6

"Imagine not having to cover up what is true about you. Imagine receiving the gifts of grace that God has given you in order to heal the unresolved issues in your life. . .That's where we're headed."

-Behind the Mask

FEBRUARY

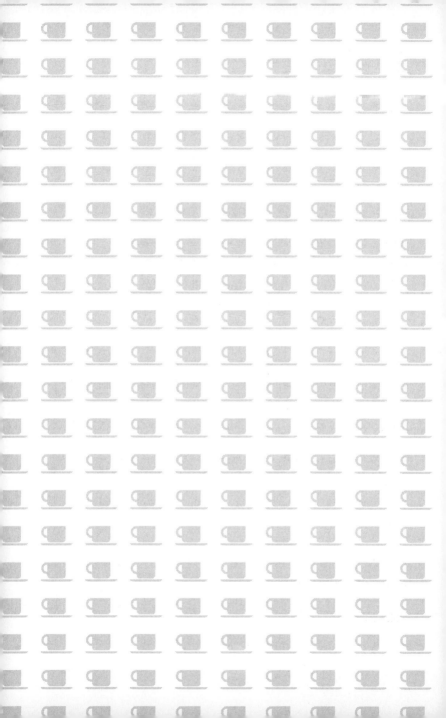

THREE BASICS OF GRACE

People often ask, "What pillars does Trueface believe are essential to the gospel of grace?"

Three things. First, every major religion, except Christianity, is based on performing-for or pleasing their deity. We want you to leave that road of pleasing your deity, and take the road of trusting God, which is how you met Jesus in the first place. Millions of Christ-followers remain on that dead-end road of performing for God. He already performed for you!

Second, "humility is trusting God and others with me." If you act on this, you will begin to believe who God says you are, instead of believing who you say you are. God says you are righteous, holy, and a saint. This changes everything!

Third, humility actually attracts (doesn't earn) God's grace. Grace alone can overcome your shame, can help you work on annoying true things about you, and nurture authentic environments of grace through your life. So powerful!

Applying these three truths will produce hundreds of healing and freeing applications in your life.

Colossians 2:8

DECISION MAKING

You may be reading this on a couch in the living room. Everyone's asleep. You have a big decision to make and aren't sure what choice would please Him most.

If you've put your hope in Jesus, you have the Holy Spirit living within you. He guides you into all truth. You are not in violent disagreement with what God wants for you. If your option is not immoral, evil or illegal, God can pull off His perfect will in whatever you decide. He is not wringing His hands.

Given your new identity, the desires of God's heart are similar to the ones He has placed in you. Yes, we always need counsel. Yet, whether that decision is moving to Baltimore or Atlanta, staying put in this company or taking a promotion in that one, the question is the same: What would you like to do? God is that sovereign and you are that fused with Him.

Now, get off the couch and go back to bed. You'll need some sleep for what's up ahead.

John 16:13

LONELINESS

Loneliness is often associated with the word "new"—a new job, a new community. It usually recedes as you discover friends. But when you experience loneliness in a crowd of friends, it's often because you're wearing some kind of mask.

If you wear masks because you're not certain the real you is worth knowing, then even when it appears you are enjoyed, you're not certain they're enjoying the real you. "If they really knew me, they wouldn't like me. Because I know me, and I don't much like me."

God's assessment is crucial here. He not only loves you but *likes* you. For each of us, that liking is *unique*. He believes you are likeably and wonderfully made. You just have to believe that He believes that. Then you can walk into any situation, new or familiar, in humble confidence: "God thinks I'm worth knowing. So someone here is liable to think that too."

And the old howl of loneliness will begin to fade in your new found freedom. You are likeably and wonderfully made.

Psalm 139:13-14

STOP, LOOK, AND LISTEN

So life has thrown you something that seems impossible for God to fix. Almost immediately, you'll be tempted to try to protect yourself.

Before you do, stop and look: When you stare back, God really looks good, doesn't He? He's gotten you through it all. You're reading this, so you're still here, after some pretty dicey situations. Now listen: Those are the sounds of you praising Him for His faithfulness. There were many times when you thought He couldn't come through. But He did.

With so much life already in the book, it's clear: God can handle whatever comes at you. He's even planned ahead for the curveballs you haven't seen yet.

So, back to that thing life threw your way. Why not face what's in front of you, betting He'll probably figure this one out too?

Lamentations 3:22-23

THE MORALISTIC SHAME FILTER

They are the same words, but if you read the scriptures through a filter of shame or moralism you can interpret them very differently from their intent. John 14:15 says, "If you love Me, you will keep My commandments." If you doubt you can maintain enough love for God, then this verse is frightening. If you're convinced you must keep enough commands to stay saved, this verse is terrifying!

But as you begin to trust God's love, you can gradually take off those filters. It's like scales falling from someone's eyes. It's freeing to discover that "if" is a first-class conditional conjunction in the original language—an *if of certainty*. It might read, "Because." It's also a great joy to discover that Christ's "commandments" are all applications of one command, which we *can* fulfill—His new command, John 13:34, to "love one another."

That previously alarming verse is now clear: "Because you love Me, you'll find yourself longing to keep my commandments. It's what you desire to do most of all."

Romans 13:8-10

DEPENDENCE AND FIXING

Your best life is not the pristine life, the fixed life, the neatly ordered life. Your best life is the real one—with God receiving glory as you trust and enjoy Him and others, in the good and in the unresolved.

To fix everything is not to care for you. To give you what you envy of others is not to love you well. To heal every infirmity may not allow you to learn dependence upon Him or enter into compassion for others. Life without depending on Him will never satisfy your heart or allow His glory to be revealed in you.

You have the privilege today, even in the midst of what does not change and only seems to get worse, to walk in His real best. God is moving you and your circumstances in perfect timing.

In the meantime, remember that everyone is experiencing beauty and rubble. You get to be their fan. You can be a gift to many as you risk living your best life.

Simply stay present to it all. God's got this.

Isaiah 50:10

A GOOD CUP OF COFFEE

Some people just drink coffee. They don't care if it's from a pot in a convenience store or burned from sitting all morning. After all, it's *just* coffee.

Others, perhaps you, demand something more. The beans, water, process, and everything surrounding it must be done exactly so. *Or it's not really coffee*. For you, coffee equates to self-care.

Now, place yourself in the perfect setting for that cup of coffee. Invite the ideal friends who'd enjoy a perfectly brewed cup as much as you.

What does that feel like?

You might use words like "serenity," "peace," "warmth." All is well with the world.

Nothing profound here, only this: Jesus enjoys this setting and experience as much as you do.

He even enjoys those folk who think it's *just* coffee. It's who He is.

Ecclesiastes 5:18-20

CONVERSATIONS JESUS MIGHT HAVE HAD

(*Walking with His disciples along the Kidron Valley*)

Philip: "Jesus?"

Jesus: "Yes, Philip?"

Philip: "That water You made into wine. It was so good! I'd never had wine like that before. Will You do that again sometime?"

Jesus: "Probably not. That one was to honor my mom. And to remind her that while I am her son, I am also the Son of Man."

Philip: "Hands down the best wine I've ever had. The best any of us have ever had."

Jesus: "Yeah, well, just wait until the French show up."

Philip: "The who?"

Jesus: "The French. They'll teach your children's children about macarons, soft cheese, baguettes, duck. And they'll produce a Cab Franc that'll make what I produced at the wedding taste like Snapple."

Philip: "Snapple?"

Jesus: "Yes. And I'd appreciate it if you didn't share this with the others."

Philip: "Sure."

This is the last time the matter was spoken of. But every now and then he and Jesus would nod knowingly to each other.

John 21:25

THE POWER OF LOVE

If we work on our sin, it does not mean that we will learn to love. If we work on learning to give and receive love, we will not only love more but we will also sin less.

Those two sentences must be wrong. Right? Most of us were taught that if we worked on our sin, then somehow we would become more morally upright Christians. Learn to sin less and you're a better, more loving person. *Voila!*

Yeah, and all those children who didn't adopt their parent's faith? They noticed that didn't work.

Christ in us means that we contain love. Instead of trying to drum up an external love, we learn to trust that love is now indigenous. Counting on that to be true releases that love to others.

Romans 13:8-10 is clear: "Love does no wrong to a neighbor; therefore love is the fulfillment of the law."

If we could create communities whose goal was to learn to love and receive love, from God and from humans, the faith-attrition rate in our children and children's children would go down dramatically. For love works.

Romans 13:8-10

WHEN YOU DON'T WANT TO GO TO CHURCH

No, you don't have to go.

But a community of faith can be a place where you find hope and God's presence in the midst of flesh and blood. You can learn everything a preacher has to say online, but if you don't go, then you can't sit shoulder to shoulder with those struggling to believe, those very different from you, those who know you really well. And you can't experience the power of staying in a safe place when you need to be known—or when you want to hide.

Now if you find yourself in a place preaching moralism to keep God happy, then feel free to stay home and invest in your own way to enjoy God for a time.

But keep on the lookout for a community risking the truths of grace. Go, even if the preaching is mediocre and the drums can be a bit loud. A community where you get to live out love together, trying out the truth of "Christ in us"? Go for it.

Psalm 133

THE DISTINCT PRIVILEGE OF LOVERS

The very image of God is placed uniquely into each human—even in the roughest, most vile people in history. Think Mussolini or Jezebel, or your no-good-crazy-ex.

When they were kids, if only briefly, they dreamed of how that image of God in them could be lived out, even if they had no clue it was *His* image. Then things got sideways. Some of that is due to their environment, some of it genetics, some their own choices.

It is the distinct privilege of lovers to call out the image of God in others—not just polite folk, but even the ones who arrogantly and intentionally cause harm to others.

It's what we get to do with our lives. It is the payoff for trading away self-absorption for grace.

Sometimes a Saul of Tarsus, carrying the image of God, doesn't yet know what to do with it. God uses a grace-filled Ananias to point to a new name, a new life, and a new vision.

It's what lovers do.

Acts 9:1-19

GRACE IS NOT . . .

Grace is not a pass I give myself. Or a demand to let me off the hook after I've wronged you. Or self-entitled permission to get my way.

Grace is never a way of living that is less passionate, less sincere, less caring, or less alive. Grace is never freedom to "play around the edges." Grace does not desire to win over another theological system. Grace is not simply a theological system. Grace is not something I talk you into. It's not something only certain people "get." Grace doesn't want to read less or pray less.

Grace is not just to get me to heaven. Grace is not for inferior Christians. Grace is not a crutch. Grace is not freedom to drink more or do just enough. Grace is not to be balanced with anything. Grace does not balance. Grace is not an afterthought of God after we sinned in the garden. Grace is not merely graciousness. Grace is infinitely more than any attempt to manipulate it.

Romans 6:1-7

GRACE IS . . .

Grace is the means for living every moment of my life. Grace is the only way to face my sin. Grace is how the Trinity relates to each other, and the basis for our relationships. Grace allows me to believe my righteousness. Grace convinces me I'm a new creature, loved as much as any other creature on Earth. Grace frees me to stop striving.

Grace removes the pressure to be enough and convinces me I am enough. Grace draws me like a child to Jesus. Grace gives me the gift of repentance and woos me to forgiveness.

Grace allows me to laugh and relax without looking over my shoulder. Grace anticipates my failure yet won't let me stay there. Grace causes me to want to do the hard works of love. Grace lets me enjoy my life and not feel guilty about it.

For much of Church history, grace was primarily understood for justification by grace through faith. We may be entering a reformation of sanctification by grace through faith.

Colossians 2:6

GRACE CAN . . .

Grace can release me from tiresome religious duty to contagious contentment, delight, and purpose. Grace can free me from trying to "one up" others. Grace can take away trite and corny religious humor.

Grace can redirect my anger into concern. Grace can release dormant love. Grace can reduce depression, angst, fear, and doubt. Grace can magnify my enjoyment of God.

Grace can take away uncertainty of my eternal destiny. Grace can cause me to want to be right for the right reasons. Grace can take away man-made taboos and restrictions. Grace can make me kinder. Grace can inspire me to offer grace. Grace can cause me to work harder than by any other means. Grace can reduce my insecurities. Grace can cause me to acknowledge my unhealthy responses. Grace can redirect an entire community. Grace can heal an unhealthy church.

Grace can begin to bring reconciliation to generations of old divisions of race, religion, and gender equality. Grace can redirect an entire nation.

John 1:14-17

GRACE
CANNOT . . .

Grace cannot be improved upon. Grace cannot take sin more seriously. Grace cannot be ignored just because some have misunderstood and mis-taught it.

Grace cannot and will not let me down. Grace cannot be insufficient. Grace cannot cause me to take advantage of God. Grace cannot cause me to hurt God's heart. Grace cannot be matched by moralistic technique or striving self-effort. Grace cannot be indifferent to the pain sin causes me and others. Grace cannot be bothered with false teachers who claim it is not enough.

Grace cannot be satisfied with my justification. Grace cannot be limited to Christians. It is available when anyone calls upon it for salvation. Grace cannot stop smiling at what it sees for my future. Grace cannot be derailed by my failure. Grace cannot be stopped by misfortune or calamity. Grace cannot be taught enough. Nothing is more needed in my time of need. Nothing can strengthen my heart more than the grace of Jesus. Nothing.

1 Peter 4:10

THE BEST BIBLE IS . . .

There are dozens, yea verily, hundreds of Bible translations, paraphrases, and transliterations (whatever that means). There will be no end to the people telling you which is the one God wants you to read. Some will shame you for reading that paraphrase whose name rhymes with "The Cressage."

The best Bible though is the one you'll read. There are many excellent online sources that can help you with difficult passages to make sure you're getting the sense of the original. So, knock yourself out! Use the app on your phone, or buy a Bible with a waterproof cover. It's like buying a comfortable pair of running shoes to make the experience optimum. The Bible wasn't meant to be hard. Most of the verses mean exactly what they appear to mean. The rest are for people with tassels on their hats to debate over.

Remember, the best Bible is the one you'll read. Then of course you'll need to figure out if you want your name engraved on it.

Psalm 119:17

PRACTICING SUBMISSION

Submission. It simply means to come under the influence of another. Because some have violated it as a control word, we can miss that submission is really a love word. So we may fake it, with either compliance or appeasement. But submission to another who has strengths where I have weaknesses allows me to get the best the other has to offer. Submission displays the humility that you're convinced you cannot direct yourself well without others. Submission honors others by expressing that they've earned your trust.

There is another, less obvious benefit to your submission. Others are watching you. They are considering if you are someone *they* should let influence them. Their "letting" is submission. Your visible submission to others signals that you are the real deal and that it may be safe to come under your influence.

Submission has gotten a bad rap by those who have tried to manipulate it for power and control. True submission will not be manipulated. When it is experienced, many core needs of people are met in relationships of love.

Ephesians 5:21

BEING WINNABLE

The stats on parenting and baseball hitting are similar. Even the best seem to get it wrong a lot more than right.

But our kids would tell us it's less important that we get it right than being winnable when we don't. They are wired for our mistakes. What they're not designed for is when we pull rank and won't fess up.

Ever said this? "When you're older, you'll understand I was right." Or, "I'm the parent. I decide what's right around here!"

You may win that battle, but at the risk of losing their hearts.

The ability to tell on yourself is endlessly spendable currency. If you're sincere, your kids will trust you. You may think, "But if I do that, they won't respect me." If you don't, then while they might comply with you, their respect will fade.

You will make plenty of mistakes. Just make sure, when you hurt them, that you tell them, "Hey, that was about me. Will you forgive me?"

They'll trust and respect that you chose to admit when you were wrong.

Proverbs 25:12

PROXIMITY

The FBI has offered a five million dollar reward for the return of Rembrandt's *The Storm on the Sea of Galilee*. The painting was stolen from the Isabella Stewart Gardner Museum in Boston on March 18, 1990.

The painting is astonishing. Find a version of it online. It captures the disciples at various heart conditions in the midst of the violent, sudden storm. Some cling to the mast. Some desperately adjust the rigging (as though that will do anything). One gave up, wrapped himself in a blanket, and awaits imminent death. One vomits over the side. A few sit closer to Jesus. Those farther out listen to Him but clearly watch the storm. Several are right beside Him, concerned, but stare directly into the eyes of Jesus.

Rembrandt has artfully captured a profound truth. We have no independent ability to solve any life issue. We have one thing we can do: stay close to Jesus and let Him love us. That's doable. It takes no more than believing He's in control of the storm.

Mark 4:35-41

WHEN YOU'RE YOUNGER

When you're younger it can feel like there's no one who sees life like you do. You sit in church groups feeling like you're at a convention of aliens whose language you're not familiar with. You watch couples in the park, or friends laughing in restaurants. You think, *Where's my crowd? I feel like a visiting guest everywhere I go.*

Some people just make friends quickly. Others need time. You will find your crowd. But you have to be willing to let yourself be found. This is risky. You'll get hurt, betrayed, not picked, left behind, made fun of, and a hundred other possibilities. But one day, you'll be surprised. They'll like you for exactly who you are. God's been preparing this: *friends*.

Psalm 139:1-18

DOING RIGHT VS. BEING RIGHT

When conflict has stalled a relationship, *it's always more important to do right than to continue to promote that you are right.* Even if you are technically right, you may end up being right by yourself.

The truth you're promoting is probably important, maybe vitally important. But another dynamic is compromising the truth you're holding tightly to. A relationship has become strained. A truth has been clouded by holding to that position with all your might. You've made your right position more important than the relationship, demanding the other see your way before you move forward. Your demand can feel to them like arrogance, stubbornness, or lovelessness.

God's not asking that you change your view of truth. He's asking that you discover another truth: when one chooses humility, heart change can move faster and easier.

2 Timothy 2:23-26

GROWN-UP MOTIVATION

You were raised to do right. But you're grown now. Finally it's your life, and no one's looking over your shoulder. You're suddenly filled with feelings and thoughts you've never had before. A lot of what you've been told was wrong actually feels very right.

Here's some grown-up motivation. While you'll always be forgiven, you'll be shaped by what you choose. If you take what or who does not belong to you, it'll twist you. It'll take real time to untwist that. It's hugely important now to study what God thinks. He holds the best life. He intends no second-class life for you. He knows how to give stunning joy and pleasure that doesn't harm. You'll also discover a motive in your heart that wants to experience intimacy with God. You have God in you! He can be accessed to fight wrong. You have real power inside you.

Keep going. You have quite the life ahead of you!

Proverbs 4

GRACE FOR ALL

Joseph Cooke wrote, "Grace is the face love wears when it meets imperfection." When grace shows up, the setting is often pretty messy. Sanitized and polished appearance has little room for grace.

Grace seeks out imperfection, runs to it. Grace is all over the face of the prodigal's father as he rushes to his son. Grace isn't only for the weak, as though they were a people group. Grace is for the older son in the story who will need the love of grace in his bitterness. Grace is for all. We are at once flawless and flawed, pure and impure, holy and full of holes, righteous and not in our right mind.

When all their best plans for how life should work broke, both sons needed grace to meet them in their imperfection. We may recognize grace when it shows up. We may not. Grace makes a space for the truth to be told and heard, even if it's painful. Grace makes a place for people to find themselves whole again right in the middle of falling apart.

2 Corinthians 9:8

GOD AND HUMOR

Do you ever wonder about humor? You know, laughter and all that? Like in Genesis, when old Sarah found out she was going to have a son and she just cracked up?

Can self-effacing humor defuse another's mistrust? Can you actually be seen as more known and trustworthy through humor? How long would we really make it if nothing was funny? Do angels laugh when we say something funny?

Do people who laugh a lot live longer? In heaven, will we be able to make God laugh?

Does another's ability to laugh cause us to trust them more? Do the evenings we will remember most involve a lot of great and safe laughter? Does maturity sometimes express itself by employing humor that builds up and doesn't mock? Can humor actually heal and free? Is the ability to enjoy humor one of God's most delightful gifts to us?

Does God love the sound of your laugh? Like, could it be on His list of favorite things about you?

Psalm 126:2

TAKING OFF MASKS

Maybe you've come to understand you've been wearing a mask for most of your life. So, what now?

Maybe you start with the sad reality that there's not just one mask. There's a variety, one for each occasion. But here's great news about you: You're no longer bluffing about your bluffing. You're also coming to understand that you can't take off the masks by technique, self-effort, or contrition.

The mask comes off only when you're convinced the real you is worth knowing.

You are not your sin. You are not your past. You are not your wrong choices. You are not your upbringing. You are not your addictions. You are not your size, height, weight, or attractiveness. You *are* Christ in you. The God of the universe stands with His arm around you every moment, sleeping or waking. Clinging to this will dissolve the glue affixing the masks to your face. This alone will allow you to be comfortable in your own skin.

This alone will allow you to show your true face.

Romans 8:18-21

IS GOD TRYING TO "BREAK" YOU?

I think people often hear, "God needs to break you."

But, what if Jesus came to heal you? What if you're already broken? He doesn't need to break you more in order to heal you.

Imagine Jesus saying this to you: "How could you ever allow your heart to rest in One who, at any moment, would unleash something intended to break something in you? Please understand, child, you came to Me broken, devastated, undone, shattered and bleeding. Every moment of anything I've allowed, denied, withheld or caused has been to undo the damage that has already been done—both to you and by you. Yes, pain and confusion will hit you. It is the result of living on this planet. It hits every human. I am sovereign and love you even more than you do. I am even able to control what pain gets through. Yes, there is discipline from love. But there is never even a hint of retribution or punishment. Ever."

Luke 11:11

A MINT ON THE BED (PART ONE)

It's funny when those who seek stuff, dwell on stuff, pout when they don't have stuff, envy those with stuff, and manipulate their world to get stuff, seem to enjoy it least when they finally get it. It's just like those who seek status and position and are willing to sacrifice priorities of family or their intimacy with God to get it, but once they've arrived have little or no joy.

Jesus gives an extraordinary secret to life when He implores us to drink in the kingdom of God and His righteousness. He promises that a quality of life beyond what we even knew to ask will come around, in one form or another, and be better than what we could have designed in our limited imagination and perspective.

There's only one stipulation: You'll have less control over the exact specifications of what you get. But it won't really matter. Experiencing God's presence in a Motel 8 is superior to the sense of God's absence in a hotel where you get a mint on your bed.

Matthew 6:33

A MINT ON THE BED (PART TWO)

Okay, so it won't matter if we'll have less control over the exact specifications of what we get. But what if we could have God's presence, His delight, *and* a mint on the bed! Shouldn't we pursue that?

Enjoy God and make choices when they're presented that display your taste and preferences.

But just know:

- If you pursue the mint on the bed, it may not taste as good as you had hoped.
- If you pursue God, you may, at some time, find yourself in a place with a mint on your bed and it will taste really, really good. And you'll receive the added delight of knowing that its goodness came not from the mint but from the very hand of God.
- If you choose to delight in Him, those times without the mint on the bed will often be the ones you'll remember and cherish the rest of your life.

Matthew 6:33

"Permission to the heart is earned. Always."

-The Cure and Parents

MARCH

TRUTH AND DARE

"To the exact extent that the Father loves Me, so also I love you" (paraphrase of John 15:9).

This is a doozy of a statement by the Son of God. Essentially, the exact amount God loves Jesus is the same amount Jesus loves you. Yeah, you. Sure, you agree the words are true. But can you dare to believe they could possibly be true about you?

Before you're ten minutes out your door, life will try to give you a dozen reasons to believe that Jesus must have been speaking of someone else.

The only way you will ever experience the magnitude of this love is to embrace it apart from your erratic behavior. Jesus absolutely delights in you. Yeah, you.

Every time life throws your unworthiness at you, pause and remind yourself that this distinctive, unchanging love He has for you is independent of anything you might say or do. Then dare to believe it, and spend the rest of your day amazed.

Ephesians 3:17-19

MATURING

The Holy Spirit is orchestrating our transformation.

It's like the activation of yeast. You add ingredients and then trust what you cannot see.

What you *can* see clearly along the way are your failures, your intermittent good choices, and your immaturity. It's all okay.

Your primary role is to trust. You trust the Holy Spirit and others with you. You believe you really are this new creation with a heart that can be trusted. You believe you can replace unhealthy patterns with healthy decisions. You realize you can live lovingly for the benefit of others. You refuse to hide. You learn the art of enjoying God because you want to, not because you must. You come to believe you are actually righteous, even when your behavior screams you are not.

Gradually, you recognize that the Spirit's fruit is increasingly flourishing in you and through you to others.

It is happening. As predictably as yeast rising to fill a room with the aroma of goodness, the undeniable maturing of Christ in you fills the room.

Ephesians 4:13

GRACE IS A GAME-CHANGER

Some believe the truths of grace are nice, unless you're in a field of high performance and winning. That atmosphere demands a harsher form of motivation. But consider this.

Joe Maddon managed the 2016 World Champion Chicago Cubs. He was serious about changing the beliefs of how winning best takes place.

Maddon said, "I don't want my players afraid of making mistakes."

An authoritarian coach believes he wins by keeping his players under control, motivating them by rewards or threats. It's all rigid and highly impersonal.

Maddon managed with humility, authenticity, candor, and sometimes playful absurdity. He chose to see athletes differently, through the eyes of grace.

The cycle of authoritarian coaches won't change completely. Athletes are conditioned by authoritarian coaches from Little League forward. When they become coaches themselves, they simply model the behavior of the coaches they remember.

But there are those, like Joe Maddon, who've risked breaking that cycle. Grace works in every life situation, even with the boys of summer. Amazing, isn't it?

Colossians 3:12-14

WHEN SOMEONE LEAVES YOU

Nothing can cause you to question your very being more than someone you love choosing to leave—divorce, your first real love, or a friend you thought would always stay. It undoes you.

At such times the poets and the singers seem to say it best. They choose words like "heartache" and "heartbroken." That feels about right.

Hebrews's writer quotes God's heart particularly to you, as if no one else was on the planet: "I will never desert you, nor will I ever forsake you."

"I will never . . . nor will I ever . . ." God's promises are often like depth charges. When you're wonderfully in love and your heart's on fire, they may not matter as much.

But suddenly, when you've forgotten your name and your way home—*Boom!*—God stands directly in front of you, saying, "Look at Me. I won't leave. Not for a moment or an inch. I'm here for the entire rest of forever. When you risk loving another again, I'll still be right here."

Deuteronomy 31:6

TO BE LOVED

What does it mean to be loved? You might fear it is a gushy, vague, almost unwanted and cloying thing.

But to be loved is to be known. Of course you might fear *that*. For you know yourself too well.

But what if you were known by Someone who cared more about you than you care about yourself? What would *that* be like? Someone who knows everything about you and will not use it against you? Someone who calls attention to you and your good work, even when your motive is primarily but not completely healthy?

That Someone is Christ. And as a believer, you have Christ in you. You are a new creation, otherwise known as "Christ in you!" You are fully known and completely loved, but not in some syrupy greeting-card kind of way. No, this is strong love, willing to move heaven and Earth and sacrifice everything and then some for you.

This is what scripture refers to as "perfect" love, the kind that drives out fear and never, ever abandons us.

1 Corinthians 1:25

TO LENT OR NOT TO LENT

In the tribe of grace are those who celebrate Lent and those who don't. For some it is sacred. For others it feels contrived. Some find it a beautiful vehicle to express their adoration of a God who has carried their sins and freed their hearts. Others don't. Some experience God transcendently in liturgy, symbolism, and the senses evoked by smell, touch, taste—even denial. For others anything more formal than talking to God on a walk is religious annoyance. Some reach back into the historic faith of the Church. Others have a hard time relating to the uneven history of the Church.

We honor each other by remembering that nobody owns the market on best practices. There is bad religion all over the world, on both sides of the liturgical aisle. We want to offer hope without tearing down people. Tearing down usually just tears down trust. Free people are privileged to honor the dignity of other free people even when they don't agree.

Colossians 2:16-17

NODDING

Have you ever thought about the impact of a simple nod?

A study was published in the scientific journal *Perception*. A group watched videos of people nodding, or not nodding, then rated what they thought. A nod makes you about one-third more likable and 50 percent more approachable. The study confirms how much we need validation!

If love is the process of meeting needs (and it is), and if affirmation is an act of love that meets a need (and it is), then one way of loving another is simply by nodding.

Your nod doesn't necessarily mean you agree. It might say, "I'm not sure I agree with what you're saying at the moment, but I delight in you, the person I'm looking at, very much."

The study's value is in showing us one of the gestures love naturally expresses to give another value: nodding.

Imagine what it would be like to experience Jesus nodding as you speak?

Though you can't see it, He's nodding now, at you.

1 Peter 4:8

WORRY

Jesus says in Luke 12:22, ". . . do not worry about your life."

But it can feel irresponsible to not worry, especially about important things happening to us and to those we love.

Worry can be defined as the "mental distress or agitation resulting from concern for something impending or anticipated." So how do we just not worry? Matthew 6:32 says ". . . but your Father knows that you *need* these things." The God in control of the universe, who loves us more than we love ourselves, more than we love those dearest to us, *that* One knows our needs.

That mental distress over the impending? That's not ours to carry. Our God chooses to carry it. So, cast "all your anxiety on Him, because He cares for you."

1 Peter 5:7

TRUTH AND CONSEQUENCES

Many children, early on, discover that the consequences for telling on themselves are the same as for getting caught. So they try to perfect the art of not getting caught.

When they do get caught, the punishment convinces them to never tell on themselves. This creates a vicious cycle between parent and child.

Some parents are learning to throw a wrench into that cycle. The wrench is grace. They're convincing their children to tell on themselves when they fail and that the outcome will be different than if they get caught.

When our children believe us and begin to tell on themselves, magic happens—but only if the parent is able to follow through with a response that honors the child's vulnerability.

This kind of parenting can set in motion vulnerable relationships of honesty. Hiding starts to vanish, along with that lingering unspoken darkness that fills the air in an environment of deceit. There is definitely a learning curve for both parent and child. But even if it's clumsy, it is life-giving.

1 John 1:7-9

THE WET WOOLEN COAT

Some people wake up singing "What a Wonderful World." But there are countless others who don't wake to music of any kind. They fight hard simply to stand up, get dressed, and walk out the door. They don't really want to. There is sadness all over them, like a wet woolen coat they can't seem to shake.

If that's how you feel or it accurately describes someone close to you, here's some truth: Jesus sees you and is proud beyond words of your choice to endure. He's walking with you, kindly saying, "I know you feel dull, uninspired, and behind. You don't have to be afraid of the thought that you're losing it. Don't try to reason with those voices. Instead, call out My name. Put on good music. Talk to Me—about anything. I've cleared My schedule just for you."

So take it easy. Breathe. This pace and lack of clarity do not define you. The best about you is embedded. It cannot be shaken. And even wet wool cannot hide it.

Romans 8:22-28

TAKE A HIKE

Sabbath comes from the Hebrew word "to cease." As in stopping from our normal work and schedules. We all need a break from our routines to restore our vision, creativity, energy, and to experience more focused joys with God. He knew this when He instituted "ceasing."

Ceasing means we have to *stop* what we are doing. Many of us are not good stoppers. We incessantly move to the next thing. Without stopping, you cannot rest. You can choose many things from which to rest, besides work. These can include resting from worry, errands, technology, multitasking, and talking.

Conversely, God's grace means you get to delight in His creation and enjoy a sense of play with Him. Pete Scazzero refers to Sabbath as like receiving the gift of a snow day every week—no obligations, pressures or responsibilities and permission to play, be with friends, read a good book, and soak in God's love. Pete says, "He gives you over seven weeks of snow days every year!" This is part of the freedom for which Christ set you free.

Psalms 46:10

CODDIWOMPLE

The verb "coddiwomple" has been popularized recently: "to travel in a purposeful manner toward a vague destination."

That describes the journeys of Joan of Arc, Moses, those from Hebrews 11, and the rest of us.

God promises to never forsake us. He asks us to risk this promise based on His character. But trusting comes with few trail markers.

Along the way, however, we do get glimpses of what He's promised. The journey is as important as the destination—God has so much more for us than just the end of the story.

This is not a road trip, where we grab a friend, and some Cheetos, and snake along backroads in search of a diner with the world's best hash browns.

Coddiwompling with God is risking our very lives. It must be why it pleases God so much. We're counting on God to give us a life worth living. We're believing He can make sense of adolescence, marriage, careers, aging parents, and all the rest. To walk purposefully in this way is not a slight thing—not a slight thing at all.

Coddiwomple on.

Hebrews 11

THE SKY IS NOT FALLING

Hi. It's Me. So, you woke up this morning feeling not right. You can't name it. Nothing from the day before. You just feel off—way off. And coffee is not helping.

Sometimes you can't find it because I'm not revealing it. I'm allowing you to be discontent with how things are. I'm maturing you. Some of the old patterns just aren't serving you well anymore.

You don't have to figure anything out. Just know the sky is not falling. It's only Me. You came to this new life deeply broken. We performed triage early on but then had to allow you to heal for a bit.

Get your legs under you. Enjoy the new you.

But you sense it. There's much yet unformed. That's why you feel off today. I'm working in you, not to harm you but to heal, mature and free you. If you could see what I'm doing, you wouldn't need coffee to skip around the house. For now, just rest in My love.

Philippians 2:13

ENJOYING YOURSELF

One of the great gifts of embracing grace is the new sensation of enjoying your own company. When you felt you never measured up with God or life, you could carry a pretty sad running background dialogue: "Where should I be? It can't be here, because here is just me. The silence is too loud. I've got to find something else to do—a shoe store perhaps."

It is a great moment to discover that God wants to be where *you* are.

Try that on for a moment. In the entire universe, somehow He wants to be right here with you. Don't let the fact that He can be several places at once throw you off.

He is absolutely delighted enjoying this moment with you!

Question His taste if you must, but apparently He really likes being with you. If all you do today is sit and read and file your nails, He's happy to keep you company—just the two of you.

It kind of gives more meaning to enjoying yourself.

1 John 4:15-16

LIFE IS EXHAUSTING.
I AM NOT.

Hello, My friend.

Today I only want to remind you of this: Life is exceedingly exhausting, but I am not. Our relationship is not to be tough. Many will tell you it's supposed to be. But it is not. In-laws can be tough. Childbirth is tough. Calculus is definitely tough. But *I* am not. I want to be your safest place. Life will try to convince you that I don't care or that I am not strong enough. But never miss this: I am for you. Some of what you experience may make no sense for a while. In the meantime hold to this: no one is more for you than Me. I am not working against you or contending with you. I want to give you life.

I know you are broken. With My entire being I am working to heal you. You will bear some pain and loss. This is the result of being alive in a fallen world. But I will turn it all into good. You have My word on it.

John 16:33

SUFFERING FOR DOING GOOD

"No good deed goes unpunished." That clever line does fit many occasions, but it's not universally true. Many good deeds are rewarded and are not accompanied by punishment, or even discomfort.

"The good often suffer opposition for doing good." That's probably the more universally true statement. Jesus suffered for doing good. Thousands more did the same, before and after Jesus.

The Father exalted Jesus and many more who trusted Him in the middle of wronged suffering. We do not create our own influence. It's given by God.

Many with title and power do not display maturity, much less wisdom. The powerful who have not been given that influence by God often coerce or even abuse followers with their position and dominance. However, the one who has suffered for doing right has matured through that season, which is why God trusts them with influence. Now, they guide through their wisdom and love.

When God calls you to suffer for doing right, and He will, remember the sacred beauty of the influence He wants to give you.

Philippians 2:1-13

SUFFERING WITH A PAYOFF

Brennan Manning wrote, "Suffering has often been the shortest path to intimacy with God." We fear these words are more true than we might like.

The mystery is deep and befuddling. But in the middle of our particular maladies, whether physical, physiological, or emotional, it can give us immense comfort—believing the goodness of God rescues us from despair and cynical unbelief.

We know ourselves. We wouldn't have chosen this route. But it turns out we crave intimacy with our entire beings. So God allows for our sorrows to not be wasted. Our suffering is not in vain.

Oh our God, please allow this confusing loss, pain, and grief to allow exactly the intimacy the scriptures say it will. Only You could figure out such a thing. Only You could take what feels like death and breathe life into it.

James 1:2-4

ORANGE BLOSSOMS AND BARBECUE

God has prepared life to come around in seasons. Memories affix themselves to seasons. Spring comes again and again, and that's especially wonderful if you live in a place with orange trees. It's hard to breathe in the scent of orange blossoms and simultaneously think about the flu or taxes.

God is at work in seasons. When you experience a comforting scent, God is communicating, "I remember those times of goodness." When you smell cinnamon, pine needles, or a thousand other aromas, past hope can be rekindled.

Aromatherapy is one of the most hopeful treatments for Alzheimer's patients. Introducing particular smells can awaken dormant places in the brain, causing memories to be aroused.

Today you may smell a neighbor's barbecue as you walk through the neighborhood. Ten years from now, you may smell that smell again and remember something good from today. Your sense of smell will borrow comfort from this day—because life comes around in seasons.

2 Corinthians 2:14-16

REJECTION

Maybe you got passed up for a promotion. Maybe someone left you for another. Maybe you got cut in the last round of JV basketball try-outs. Or maybe your proposal was returned with "Not at this time."

Rejection, in any form, can kick the wind out of you. Ultimately you got hurt because you tried something. Those who never attempt anything significant don't get rejected much. Heroes get rejected on the way to becoming heroes. Lovers often have their love rejected.

It hurts because it feels like the real you has been rejected. "For God so loved the world" is great news, but you're not the world; you're you! Rejection is individual.

There is an acceptance beyond the sting of rejection. God offers it to each of us. While given to many, God's love is individual and personal. He truly wanted a *you* on this planet. He has personal plans for you. They may not involve JV basketball or the next great novel, but they're crafted from the perfect love of God. Meanwhile, your full acceptance is secure.

Psalm 139:13-16

GRACE IN THE WORKPLACE

After falling in love with this way of life in grace, we long to try it out with our family, friends, and ministries. No place is off-limits.

Except maybe at work.

We can presume that an environment of grace is mutually exclusive to an environment of paychecks and bottom lines. The challenge of nurturing grace in the workplace is unique but desperately needed. It's possible to foster a culture of grace as an employee or employer. The elements, conditions, and convictions are largely the same for work or home.

Your boss may be totally non-relational and purely deadline-driven, seeing workers as faceless names. But *you* are there—not to rebel or undermine, but to model authenticity and safety, to encourage the potential for greater productivity as grace is expressed. Your intentionality for such an environment can become contagious. Even a non-relational department director may begin to ask questions. This is a beginning. But the first step is believing you can trust God in the workplace and that grace belongs right in the center.

Ephesians 6:5-8

SUPER POWERS

God's sovereignty is the concept that He's all powerful, able to do anything He wants. While deeply comforting, it can also feel a bit disheartening. It's comforting because He loves us and nothing evil gets by Him. Even when we experience suffering or pain, God is reshaping it for His glory and our best.

It's disheartening because it can seem like He's just going to do what He's going to do. Why pray? He knows more and has the power to turn a bowl of noodles into a velvet painting if He wants.

Our God somehow shapes what He does in concert with our asking in faith. We're learning to believe that His will is not foreign to ours. While giving up nothing of His sovereignty, He often does His will in response to our prayers. When we get to heaven, He might spend considerable time showing what He did through our requests. That's going to be a wonderful tour! Ask God the desires of your heart. You might see it again on the tour.

Colossians 4:12

ASKING YOUR KIDS

Once your kids reach five years old or so, and then for the rest of your life, consider asking your kids some version of these questions: "Do I overwhelm you? When I'm around, do you have to manage your responses? Do I sometimes frighten you or make you pretend for me?"

You'll need to modify the complexity of the questions depending upon your kids' ages. Getting a helpful response will probably depend upon you going first, so to speak. They'll want to see its not some set-up. But if you stay at it, and if they become convinced its safe, then authentic relationship might begin to bloom.

If you prove "winnable" to even their sometimes blunt responses, your kids might start to become less rehearsed around you. You might lose getting some things done via intimidation, power, loudness or control, but you'll begin to experience their sense of safety around you. You will get to be you with your kids while they get to be themselves. As trust develops, the battles subside and the mutual joys become more frequent. It's beautiful.

Colossians 3:21

SWINGING TOO HARD

Think golf or baseball or tennis. Now, true or false? The harder you swing, the farther the ball goes.

False. You might think true, but the swing actually begins to lose its shape the harder you muscle it. The bat or racket path begins to ripple and wobble, lessening the chance of powerfully efficient impact. The trick to power (apart from launch angle) is relaxed, timed smoothness.

Hmmmm. Not a bad analogy to life. Any mature believer might tell you that striving to do anything meaningful for God actually lessens your chance of efficient, powerful impact. The means of doing anything of value is relaxing in His ability, trusting His timing, while still putting in the time and intentionality. In other words, don't swing so hard. Consider backing off on self-driven intensity today in every area of your life. You might be amazed how far you go.

Galatians 3:1-5

CHRONIC PAIN

Chronic pain can make a coward of you—at least, at times. Pain that rarely subsides can steal your hope, joy, confidence, focus, and objectivity. In the middle of this soul-draining ill health, your faith is never on trial. God is never trying to see how much you can endure before your faith is proven fake. He plays no such games. When God tests, it's to reveal the gold in us He knows He started with.

No one can fully explain chronic pain, but for certain we know He'll not waste a moment of it. There will be, all along, times when His power in you will display heroic and transcendent strength to stay vitally in the moment. You will be caught off-guard in experiencing what would not be naturally possible. It may fill you with indescribable joy, surpassing what could have been experienced and given away had the chronic pain never arrived. It's no defense for chronic pain. But still, God's beauty shapes us through it, and many agree they wouldn't trade it.

1 Peter 1:6-7

CORPORATE WORSHIP

How does anyone ever worship publicly? There's endless distraction. We can't help staring at other people, perhaps worshipping differently than we do. We may admire their sense of abandonment to God, but it may not be our cup of tea. We even distract ourselves.

We're doing stuff we'd do nowhere else. Imagine raising your hands and swaying in front of a loan officer.

And the lyrics. You don't want to sing "Holy Spirit, fall afresh on us." What part of the Holy Spirit has not *already* freshly fallen within us?

But then you catch yourself. God is delighted with this platform ensemble trying their best to get out their adoration of Him. *He loves it all.* Even our self-conscious expressions, which sometimes seem almost hypocritical. He asks us to do it together. He loves that we would even try—especially if we aspire to live these words during our work week. After a while, we settle in and cherish that we were found by Him. For moments at a time, we worship.

John 4:24

FORGIVENESS (PART ONE)

Your friend hurt you and won't own it. Now you're guarding from admitting it. You don't want to give them such power. But now the pain's too loud.

You've asked others for help, to pray for you. But really you want allies. Truth is, none of it is working. You're still miserable.

As the victim, you can get hurt twice: first by the hurt, and then by the hurt you cause yourself.

Ready or not, here's the truth: *You must admit your pride*. God protects the humble and sits on His hands until the prideful one gets tired enough. You apparently decided to defend and vindicate yourself because God was taking too long.

The moment you take over, something like hooks embed themselves into you. Until you face your pride, they won't be coming out. True, it doesn't seem fair; after all, you're the one who got hurt. Why is it suddenly about your pride?

For now, ask yourself if you took over and stopped trusting God.

This is the beginning of humility.

Psalm 23

FORGIVENESS (PART TWO)

Forgiveness is the antidote God gives for the one who gets hurt. Repentance is the antidote God gives for the one who hurts another.

Often, we're the first to hurt another, and we need to repent. Sometimes, another hurts us first and we choose to not forgive. Now we've created two assignments: first to repent for not forgiving, and then to forgive.

But it is imperative to define this repentance.

Repentance isn't a promise from you to God but a gift from God to you.

Repentance is admitting you can't do anything about your sin. It's admitting you need what God did for you at the cross, applied to this very moment. Every act of repentance depends upon this act of redemption.

Receive the gift and God will show up in the moment to rescue you from yourself. Now you can get back to life and love.

You could actually employ this repentance right now. You'll never regret it.

Acts 5:31

FORGIVENESS (PART THREE)

We are used to a horizontal attempt at forgiveness. We each say we're sorry and move on, but inside we may still be wishing the other would fall down a deep dark well. This is faux forgiveness.

A vertical forgiveness needs to take place first. It does not let the other off the hook. This is for us, to release us from our hooks.

We were not created to play judge and jury with anyone's sin. Trying to leaves us sick. God frees the humble, as in those who trust Him with the sins of others. So a vertical forgiveness says, "God, I'm handing this person and what they did over to You. Only You are the judge and jury. I trust that You will vindicate me and protect me, in Your time. I am forgiving this person for each individual harm they have done to me. Please, God, I am so frightened and weary of carrying this."

In that moment, the hooks come out. This is freedom—the grace and love of God in action.

2 Corinthians 2:7

FORGIVENESS (PART FOUR)

One of the finest indications you have forgiven another is that you now long to see them freed and healed from their guilt. Because you and God are wonderfully reconciled, you have no need to see the other person grovel. *This is the love of Christ being revealed for all to see.*

You have forgiven vertically for your benefit. You now get to forgive horizontally for theirs.

Christ forgave us everything. But He allowed us to repent before He bestowed its effect. In the same way, we forgive for their sake, as they repent. Yes, we forgive freely; but if we bypass the opportunity for them to repent, then we leave them stuck in their guilt.

We allow them to stumble through words like this: "I harmed you in these ways. I want you to know how sorry I am. Will you forgive me?"

It won't always happen. But when it does, it is as supernatural as when the hooks of bitterness were taken out of your heart.

Ephesians 4:29-32

HE KNOWS WHAT I NEED

God understands what I need.

God will ultimately take care of my world.

God is fully in control of my life.

God withholds nothing that would best fulfill me.

God made me exactly who He wanted.

God truly loves, adores, and likes me.

God has my back even more if I don't self-protect.

God keeps no score. I am completely square with Him.

God has only the motive of my best and His glory in whatever He allows or causes.

God is right in the center of my every experience, entering in totally.

Post this on your refrigerator for a few weeks. Read through it before you open the doors and stare in, looking for something low-calorie that tastes good.

Philippians 4:19-20

TRUSTED FRIENDS

God helped you find your friends. He knew that trusting them would be the key to your health, maturity, and ability to give and receive love.

Honest affirmation from friends is how we discover who we are, what we can and cannot do, and what we have to give away to the world.

True friendship is a place so safe that the terrible, horrible, no-good me can be known, and I discover that I am loved more, not less.

How big is that?

Having and being such a friend can be more valuable than any talent we possess. For if love is the process of meeting needs, then being able to receive the love of another is an indispensable means of experiencing the love of God. This includes receiving corrective truths from each other. These are harder to hear at times, but eventually they will become as freeing and fulfilling as receiving affirmation.

Don't let this day slip away without telling such a friend how incredibly important they are to you.

1 Samuel 18:1-4

"One of the beautiful truths of being a follower of Jesus is that God is your Father when you feel like it's true and when you don't, and you are a son or daughter when you run and hide and when you stay and enjoy His Presence."

-The Heart of Man

APRIL

• • • • • • • • • • • •
• • • • • • • • • • • •
• • • • • • • • • • • •

 @truefacecommunity | @truefacelife

EASTER

If it didn't happen, *you* don't happen. If it didn't happen, all of us miss the bus.

Sure, some version of you may still have happened, but not *you*—no new life inside; no Jesus within you; no friends with Jesus in them; no dreams of heaven; no hope of being able to change (*really* change); no fruits of the Spirit; no freedom from condemnation; no new song; no relationship with Jesus to call your own; no safest place in the universe, where you're fully known, perfectly loved; no new generations of faith.

If, for any reason, God did not or could not accept the sacrifice, the empty tomb would not have happened, no matter how much anyone wanted it to. But it *did* happen. All the wildly hopeful, regenerated molecules lined up exactly. All the yet-untested voltage trembled, shimmered, and exploded into resurrected life.

And *you* happened, in the same way. Death into life. He is risen. He is risen indeed!

2 Corinthians 5:14-15; 1 Corinthians 15:13-18

4.1

FAILED EXPECTATIONS

Sometimes things work out. And sometimes they don't.

Sometimes it's hard to see the intentions of God in those moments when they don't. And though weddings get rained on, and the conference speaker misses her flight connection, and a child throws up on the couch you were presenting as your mother's birthday surprise, God is working behind the scenes to honor the longings of your heart.

4.2

Here is a befuddling yet deeply comforting truth about God: He is offering something much grander than 365 days of sunshine. He is offering Himself to a world that has lost its way. He is working perfectly amidst the calamity and evil of a fallen world. Remember that every human suffers failed expectations, and this includes the weather and upset stomachs. But God is constantly reinterpreting history for His glory and your best. He loves you when things work out *and* when they don't.

Job 1:20-21

FEELING EMOTIONALLY TIRED

Emotional fatigue is not failure—or proof that you are doing life poorly. Anyone doing anything meaningful gets emotionally tired. But neglected or denied, emotional fatigue can break you down as surely as physical fatigue.

Caring costs. Being dragged into manipulative situations costs. The art of emotional health is to spend most of your currency on emotions tied to loving. This alerts you to unhealthy situations that are sapping your emotional strength. Real loving demands real and honest emotions.

Emotional fatigue doesn't get recharged by avoiding feelings. It can be replenished by allowing authentic emotion to be spent on you. Affirmation does this. A good story from a friend can do this. Resting in Christ's love through listening to music or reading does this. Spending time with any dog whose breed begins with the letter "G" (such as German shepherd or giant schnauzer or golden retriever) will most certainly do this.

It is wisdom to understand your emotions are not an endless resource but a gift that needs to be renewed.

Matthew 11:28-30

TRANSFORMATION

Truth only transforms *when* it is trusted. The implications here are staggering!

Information alone does not transform. It may educate, but if that is all it does, then you can become a well-educated person whose life is not transformed by God—for information alone cannot transform your heart. And the heart ultimately is where life change takes place.

Also, a steady diet of truth, even taught brilliantly, does not transform. Truth is important—for trusting untruth will also never transform anyone into health. Even the Bible carries little power in your life until it is trusted with your full weight.

To trust truth means to risk. Try it; let it work itself into the very way you see and do life. Convictions can be defined as truth you have come to act on.

Why not start right now? What truths from the Bible do you trust enough to risk acting on?

Trust them fully. This is the only way to build an active, living, power-filled faith that can transform not only you but generations to come.

2 Timothy 3:16-17

A LITTLE LESSON

Ants: the proverbial nuisance at picnics. Sure, they can be a pain. But we can learn a lesson from these little teachers if we have the eyes to see and the ears to hear.

In Proverbs 30, a wise guy named Agur noticed how smart the ants were to store up and prepare their food during the summer months. Why? Winter's coming. And the winter can be cold and harsh and oftentimes long.

When we think about the affirmation we receive, the *attaboy!* or *att-agirl!* or *well done!*, it's a wise idea to store those up, so to speak, in our hearts. Why? Because, just as the ants know, winter's coming and sometimes for us that means a season in our lives when the affirmations are hard to come by.

We've all had such times, and we'll have them again. During those harsh days or weeks or months, it is a grace from God to be able to remember an earlier word of affirmation to feed your heart and mind so that you can carry on.

Proverbs 30:24-28

4.5

BOREDOM

Parents often hear it a few days into the holiday or summer school break: "I'm bored!" which, if you translate from the original language, means "Entertain me!" Boredom—for some it classifies as an actual disease. We adults can be quick to criticize their inability to weather a boring day or week, and we do it while checking our phone for messages, posting a selfie on social media, or binge-watching nine seasons of a sitcom over a weekend.

"Entertain *us*!" Yeah, that's more like it.

4.6 Here's a thought: Not always, but sometimes boredom can be a gift. It can allow us the opportunity to hear God saying something about our lives or the lives of those who need us. Our problem is that we don't let ourselves get bored enough. At the first whiff of boredom, we usually scramble to fill it with activity or noise or noise-driven activity. Getting good and bored just might cause us to hear God's still small voice or pay attention to things like lilies of the field and birds of the air.

Matthew 6:25-34

IN THE CENTER OF YOUR PAIN

I always know right where you are. And I know you're hurting.

So allow Me to tell you this much: There is never a moment when you experience anything without Me in the center of it with you. Never.

And that includes pain in all of its forms and intensities.

I do not watch your pain from afar. I do not observe your pain. I experience your pain with you—maybe even more than you experience it.

4.7

I realize that telling you this does not make all the hurt go away. But I wanted you to know you're never being set up or viewed like a science experiment. Pain can lie and convince you that you are.

If you can only know, in the midst of the firestorm of unremitting agony, that I have chosen to identify Myself with you in this moment, then you may find comfort, strength, even joy.

I am here. And I'm not leaving. Ever.

Love,
God

John 11:33-35

THE GOOD HARD

One of the payoffs of trusting grace is becoming free enough from our preoccupation with guilt and shame to pay attention to loving others.

This is where it gets fun. And hard.

Some resent grace. They will say you're getting away with stuff, not taking sin seriously.

In truth, only grace can take sin seriously enough.

4.8

Loving another is hard—sometimes exceedingly hard. Humans can be very complex, confusing, caustic, careless, and clumsy. They say mean things and do stupid things. You know this because you know you.

This is where grace gets hard and exceedingly powerful. Choosing to love another involves a choice to humble yourself enough to care about another's interests even when they accuse you of the opposite.

The moralist would like you to work hard to convince others that you really care about God. Such is foolish work, keeping you from the right work. God wants you to work hard but primarily to meet the needs of others.

It is equally hard, maybe harder. It's just a right, good hard.

Matthew 5:43-44

PLACING MYSELF IN THE SCENE

Sometimes it seems the Bible reflects a galaxy far, far away.

Chew on this for a minute: Wherever you see Him in scripture responding to individuals, He's responding similarly to you.

In other words, place yourself in the scene.

When Jairus's daughter is dying, Jesus takes her by the hand and speaks deeply tender words: *talitha kum*, or "precious little girl." Because He loves each of us to the exact degree His Father loves Him, we can fully know He's offering the same compassion when we're sick.

4.9

Just as John comfortably leaned his head on Christ's chest around a campfire, knowing he had complete access to Jesus, so too you can know you have that same safety with Him! He's next to you, giving you rest from all that concerns you. As you trust that, you enter the goodness, love and safety of Jesus.

When we get Home, He'll let us see the wonder of what He was doing when we couldn't see it. We experience the love of God not far, far away, but here and now.

1 Peter 1:8

THAT VOICE IN YOUR HEAD

That running dialogue going on inside your head? Who is that?

For the most part, it's you.

God can talk to you. Even the evil one can send messages. But for the most part, it's you talking.

If you're constantly ashamed of yourself, believing God is disgusted with you, then your internal voice will reflect that. That voice can beat you up.

Occasionally, it'll show up in your outside voice. Like when you forget the papers you needed for a meeting or drop your phone on cement. "What is wrong with me? I can't believe I just did that."

Guess what? That voice can change. It'll change as you believe who you are in Christ. You will stop calling yourself a loser, or a failure, or worse.

It would be great to ask God to point out those times when you're kind to yourself, and to help your internal voice reflect His.

Your voice is changing.

Ephesians 4:13

IF I KNOW
(PART ONE)

If I know I have worth because of His choice of fully loving me, then I don't have to manufacture a reason to be loved. I can instead love you and offer encouragement.

If I know I'm loved by Him only because of His good pleasure, then I don't have to compete with you or anyone else for attention. I can instead work for your success and see your success as mine also.

If I know that I'll be taken care of by God's sovereign protection, then I don't have to preoccupy myself, scheming and pressuring myself to get ahead and do things to get noticed. I can instead look around and see who is hurting.

If I know that God is already pleased with me in Christ, then I don't have to busy myself with proving my worth. I can instead relax, play, give full attention to my family, and at the end of the day, sleep really well.

Ephesians 1

4.11

IF I KNOW
(PART TWO)

If I know that my worth in God's eyes is as fixed as the stars, then I don't have to make "success" my driving passion. I can instead let character, integrity, faithfulness, and love be my drivers.

If I know God isn't judging me by who is the best leader or who has the most authority, then I don't have to worry about positioning myself. I can instead submit to your strengths and protect your weaknesses.

4.12

If I know that God protects His dreams for me, then I don't have to worry that I've missed my destiny. When I'm free of this fear, God can use me to help foster your dreams.

If I know that I am a new creature, crucified with Christ, indwelt by the Holy Spirit, forgiven completely, justified, redeemed, and sanctified with His intimate love present each moment, then I no longer have to believe I'm disappointing Him. I can enjoy my Savior and friend every day of my life.

Ephesians 1

FREE LOVERS LOVE

We can become smug, thinking that because we can articulate freedom in Christ we've learned how to live relationally in these freedoms.

There is a theological shift from striving to trusting. But there's a surprisingly wonderful reality about freedom. Those who've experienced it become intent on protecting others who do not yet experience their freedom.

Anything less is selfish and immature. "Hey, look at me! I'm free! I do what I want!"

Great. Knock yourself out. Smoke cigars until dawn. *Then get over it.*

Sure, the Pharisee is in the corner, scribbling down notes at our party. But love is in the middle of the room, limiting its own freedoms for the weaker Christ-follower who's not quite sure yet what this new life's all about.

We're free to prove nothing to anyone. We are not free to confuse a weaker or younger sibling by flaunting behaviors that their God-given conscience has not yet given them permission to do. It can undermine their beautiful unfolding of faith.

Free lovers love. They're the most free of all.

Romans 14:13-23

4.13

CONVERSATIONS JESUS MIGHT HAVE HAD

(With Mary Magdalene, at a dinner gathering)

Mary: "Jesus? Didn't you used to build things?"

Jesus: "Yes. I was a carpenter, like my father, Joseph."

Mary: "It seems like You've stopped building things since You started hanging out with us."

Jesus: "True. All My tools are back home. I was in the middle of several projects when I got called out into the desert."

4.14

Mary: "Projects?"

Jesus: "I was working on a lazy Susan for a neighbor."

Mary: "A lazy Susan?"

Jesus: "It's hard to explain now. But one day well down the road, a child from your family line will give thanks for the food and end the prayer with "In Jesus' name" and a lazy Susan will help with what comes next. You've barely touched your food. Pass the olives and grapes across the table."

Mary: "I'm guessing a lazy Susan would help about now."

This is the last time the matter was spoken of. But every now and then she and Jesus would nod knowingly at each other.

Deuteronomy 29:29

OUR DEAR GOD

Many of us don't know how to talk to You. We hear of others praying two hours a day and we think, *What is wrong with me? Don't I love Him?* So we set a time, sit down, close our eyes—and we're lost. We manage to get a few things out that sound like a bad preacher from another century: "Oh, Thou doth fashion thine own vestibules of Thine habitations with a cornucopia of delight."

Ugh. We sound fake. We have so much to say, but we're afraid of what You'd do with our unrehearsed ramblings.

Then You bring us to our senses. You don't need us to get it right. We can make up songs that don't rhyme and You will make them rhyme to You. Nothing is off limits to talk about—doubts, fears, questions, dreams. You're big enough to handle it all. You are endlessly patient with our selfishness and petty requests.

Our dear God, help this be real.

Romans 8:26-27

4.15

SHARING JESUS IN A "POST-CHRISTIAN" AGE

The "Post-Christian" age—accurate or not, we do seem to be in a season where our non-believing friends are a little more leery of us sharing ultimate answers than they were for, say, Billy Graham. They've heard our answers a lot. Our answers are correct and must be given. But this culture appears to have hit a saturation point with our presentation.

4.16

Still many, over their loud claims of no need for God, are overwhelmed, frightened and adrift. Our best foot forward is to stand with them, without moralizing or giving platitudes—just for the sake of love, no strings. Bruce Cockburn calls us "lovers in a dangerous time."

We can show love's commitment and faithfulness when they fail. We can walk in when others are walking away. They may not want to hear about our God yet, but they are open to seeing us—*Christ in us*. Ironic, isn't it? Being loved by the God they don't want, inside the you they're learning to need.

1 Peter 2:12

WE'VE SEEN THE TEMPLATE

Some of us don't often feel His presence. We're baffled by much of what He chooses to do or not do. We don't always appreciate who He chooses to give influence to. We're left shaking our heads at who He lets into His Church. We'd have picked a very different crowd. We've watched injustice run free, and beautiful-hearted God lovers suffer abhorrently.

Yet some of us find ourselves loving and trusting Him with every fiber of our beings. We've never known love like His. He's all that is holding us together, and we know it. Whatever happens or doesn't, we're certain He'll turn it all into good. How can we possibly say that in view of all the evidence to the contrary screaming from the Internet each morning?

4.17

The cross and resurrection—we've seen the template. God took the most hideous wickedness done to the most innocent One and brought from it the highest beauty this planet has ever known. It has been more than enough to win our hearts.

Colossians 1:19-20

NEEDING TO PROVE OURSELVES

We sometimes need to prove ourselves to ourselves—to discover our capacity, what we do well, and even to reflect on our maturity—to see what God is doing in us. All of this is good.

What's not good is when we try to prove our worth to God or others. Yes, we can impress others with talent and effort. But deep down we want to be valued for who we really are, not primarily for what we can do. Ultimately, we can't be satisfied by approval from only what we do. Who you are can never be proven by impressing. Who you are is already settled by God. You are a unique creation, made in God's image, and eternally loved. When you're trying to prove yourself worthy, you've missed the point.

God is never impressed with anything you can do apart from what He does in you.

Colossians 1:25-28

A WINDOW INTO FOREVER

From the very moment we entered this life, we've known pain and tears. Some days it feels like even in heaven we'll be crying about something or other. It is almost inconceivable for us to imagine existence any other way. Life has roughed us up pretty hard.

Pause for a moment and consider the reality described in Revelation 21:4: "He will wipe away every tear from their eyes; and there will be no longer any death; there will no longer be any mourning, or crying, or pain; the first things have passed away."

It's unfathomable—the picture of God Himself wiping every tear from our eyes. It tells us that we enter eternity with tears. He could just let them dry on their own or have them disappear. Instead, one of our first moments in heaven will be God tenderly face to face with us, dabbing away our final tears.

Just imagine, instead of any other greeting, God will first deal with the tears He's been wanting to dry from the moment we were born.

Revelation 21:3-4

DISCOVERING WHO YOU ARE

It's almost impossible to discover who you are in an environment where you must perform for acceptance. There you only really learn how to become proficient at learning what others would like you to be and do. But who you really are, who God made you to be, that's all best learned in a place of safety. One of the finest gifts a parent, friend, mentor, coach, teacher or friend can offer is this safe place, where you are allowed to express yourself, ask questions about what you believe, and verbalize your preferences and what dreams you carry.

4.20

To be able to share what you think about God and not have those thoughts slapped back at you. To wonder out loud and not be scolded for your curiosity. To muse about what delights your very soul and consider what careers might best express that delight. As Paul says, "I delight in my service for God." All of this is a beautiful gift.

In such safe and beautiful places, God most readily reveals the person He's made you to be.

Hebrews 3:13

CATCHING YOUR NEIGHBOR'S FENCE ON FIRE

A couple recently had dear friends over for dinner. They'd burned wood in their fireplace hundreds of times. This time, a catclaw plant had grown to the top of their outside patio chimney. They thoughtlessly concluded it would burn off. It did, igniting a flame that quickly spread, threatening to engulf the neighbors' home, just as the fire department arrived. But that's not the big story.

This couple has many good friends, yet only a few from their neighborhood. Early the next morning, the couple started a clean-up much larger than their capacity and within minutes neighbors showed up with electric trimmers, axes, loppers, rakes, and brooms. "May we help?" The dozen just showed up, drawn to care for neighbors in need. It was ugly, hard work, tearing out thick roots of burned catclaw that ran the entire length of the adjoining backyards.

Sometimes you don't realize the love within the several blocks around you until you need it. It's a great gift to realize that God already has it in place.

Philippians 4:8

IN THE MIDDLE OF NOWHERE

A sky blanketed with intensely brilliant stars never gets old—especially if you're lying on the roof of your car with one of your kids. Maybe the kid is going through an especially tough season. You could first drive to their favorite restaurant. From there you could drive together out into the middle of nowhere, where there are no lights for miles.

If you can resist a moralizing parental speech and just be there because you want to, they will never forget that night. You'll be teaching so much by just being with them. In this way, you can express who you are for them, that you don't want to fix or solve them, that you enjoy them, that you're willing to risk their rejection. They may risk opening up to you on the ride home—or maybe not for months. But they'll figure out that you want to be the one they can talk to and trust with their heart when life gets hard. Just think about it: all that looking at stars one evening, on the hood of a car, in the middle of nowhere.

Galatians 6:2

4.22

RAIN

In much of the world, rain can be taken for granted. But in desert places, even a drizzle can elicit conversation between those who dislike each other. Recently, an unexpected rain fell for several minutes in one of those desert places of the Southwest. People walked outside as if under a spell. Some stood at attention at windows and stared past the rain. You could hear sighs. Reflective and meaningful conversations began afterward.

What's that about? C. S. Lewis wrote, "If we find ourselves with a desire that nothing in this world can satisfy, the most probable explanation is that we were made for another world." It makes you wonder if rain, among other things, like campfires, panoramic vistas, solitude, and warm donuts, draws out longing for another world for which we were made.

Who knew rain could be an apologetic for the existence of heaven?

Today, if it's not raining, you could either drive by a bakery or find a place of solitude where, if you're fortunate, you might find a taste of another world.

Job 38:25-28

4.23

HONEST THOUGHTS ABOUT LYING

Some of us grew up thinking we had to lie to survive. Maybe we didn't believe adults could handle what life was doing to us. It wasn't about right or wrong but about how good we could get at it. And we did get good at it. By adulthood we're liars. Your mom saw an ice cream wrapper in the garbage and asked how many you ate. You answered *one*. You had *five*. It was just easier to lie. We got called out sometimes, but we deflected, blamed others, or changed the subject.

4.24

Then Jesus enters the equation. We're suddenly free, alive. We don't want to hurt others with our lying. But it's like muscle memory. So we have to create *new* memory by believing who we are and experiencing what it feels like to tell the truth, even when it's costly. We're no longer defined by our lying but by new life. We will still lie at times, but we cannot stay in its shame. We own it, apologize, and move on. We are no longer liars.

Ephesians 4:17-32

BEING
OVERWHELMED

Being overwhelmed can scare us. It yells out, "This time you're probably going to be destroyed. Your only hope is to work harder and harder. Nobody can really help you. They'll just feel sorry for you. They're all doing their lives without getting overwhelmed. What's your problem anyway?" When this happens, we're often tempted to hide away from those who could protect us. Those friends are waiting to stand with us and help us work through the season.

When we get overwhelmed, we've got to stop long enough to gain objectivity. This best happens when we can get alone with God. We slow down for a moment. It feels like that'll just get us further behind, but it allows us perspective so that we can work smarter, not just harder. It reminds us that we cannot protect ourselves, that it's good to allow committed friends access to our lives.

We're once again surprised to find out they don't want to scold us or feel sorry for us. They want to help us not feel overwhelmed.

Proverbs 18:24

4.25

GENEROSITY

There is an external expression of generosity fueled by expectation, culture, and the desire to appear generous. But it is mostly thin and calculated. It extends to the door closing on you as you leave the lavish party.

Real generosity has a transcendently different vibe to it. You feel no compulsion to reciprocate. You are invited only to enjoy, with no strings attached. That is the nature of love, the river from which this generosity flows. You were re-created to receive and give this generosity. You can trust God completely with your resources. So go ahead, lose track of the score.

4.26

The generous know that they will not lose for giving more than getting. And they understand that even if they end up behind most others, they will experience the best life. God has designed it this way for all His generous lovers.

2 Corinthians 9:6-7

BACK TO PRISON FOOD

The recidivism rate, the return rate to prison, is consistently somewhere between 60 percent and 80 percent. But why would anyone go back to a place of danger, to where you don't get to freely choose your daily events, where you can't walk where you want or drive to the mountains or beach? Where you see the worst of life, eat the worst food, endure the most uncomfortable settings, amid daily violence and violation, separated from those you love?

Apparently, many believe it's scarier to live in freedom. Something in rehab didn't take. They didn't learn how to live free, in the light. Their sentence taught them only how to cope in the dark. Though horrible, at least prison was familiar. Apparently, horrible but familiar can feel preferable to free but unfamiliar.

The purpose of understanding who you are in Christ is for a rehabilitation that takes. You're not a prisoner any longer. Come out into the light. Many of us are standing with you, trying out choices in the warmth of being known.

Romans 7:21-8:4

APPARENTLY HE LIKES YOU

"For God so loved the world." That kind of obligates Him a bit, doesn't it? But after a while we begin to believe that He loves us but in sort of a universal, generalized way. We know what we've done. We know the compromise, deceit, broken promises, and meanness that exist to this day. We've trusted what Christ's forgiveness accomplished on the cross. Forgiveness is one thing, but forgetfulness? Well, that's another. You can live out your faith happy to be going to heaven while trying to just not get in the way. You make sure He knows you're pretty disgusted with yourself.

4.28

But apparently He really *likes* you. Always has. He specifically made you for His delight. He sees you as perfect and clean. He's even predisposed to enjoy your specific temperament. Seriously. His love, enjoyment, and friendship are undisturbed by your occasional erratic behaviors. The love of Jesus is that big and that mind-blowing.

Psalm 103:10-13

BAMBERG

Ascending the ancient stone steps, you crest the old city's hill onto the cobblestone square. Majestically, it towers in front of you: Bamberg, Germany's ancient cathedral.

Rebuilt in the twelfth century, it remains marvelously intact, down to the intricate statues chiseled into the mortar near the entrance.

The scenes are boldly and clearly anti-Semitic.

It is a tragically accurate depiction of much of the Church's medieval bigotry. Jewish people are portrayed as devious, moronic, and unredeemable.

4.29

It is hard to look at.

It helps frame why many generations in Europe have held to Christianity in vague name only. They weren't giving up on Jesus. They were rightly giving up on bad religion.

As proclaimers of Jesus, we get to clearly distinguish the gospel from our culture's particular version of the gospel. We get to distinguish Christianity as the antithesis of bigoted hatred. We get to offer the real Jesus, who calls out to every man, woman, and child from every language, religion, and walk of life.

He always has. He always will.

James 2:8-13

TO LISTEN IS TO OBEY

The Bible Project media team creatively reminds us that for thousands of years Jewish people have prayed "The Shema" morning and evening as a way of focusing on their God. In Hebrew the word "shema" means not only to listen, but also to respond to what you hear. In other words, to listen is to obey. Not surprisingly, in ancient Hebrew there is no separate word for obey. The team says, "In Hebrew, listening and doing are two sides of the same coin."

4.30

But something changed. Now, when you "shema", you can listen and obey from an entirely different motivation. How so? Cogent author Bill Tell shows us that in Romans 6:17 "the source of my obedience has changed . . . I 'have become *obedient from the heart*.'" This means that precisely what Ezekiel prophesied (Ezekiel 36:26) actually came to pass! God put a new spirit in you; he gave you a new obedient heart. Now, all day long, you are predisposed to shema!

Romans 6:17

"Increased devotion and diligence will not make me feel close to God again. Believing in His never-changing affection will renew my joy."

-On My Worst Day

MAY

MAY

MAKING HAPPINESS HAPPEN

Last year some friends implemented a family motto: "The Year of Making Happiness Happen." It sounded a bit presumptuous. Nobody makes happiness *happen*, right? They explained, "We love our lives and greatly enjoy each other. But too much goodness was passing us by each day. We don't want to miss it anymore. We're hoping if we talk about what brings happiness to each other, then maybe we'll find ourselves implementing it more often."

We're rarely in control of life's circumstances. But we can implement choices that can enrich happiness!

One day these friends invited other friends over to enjoy a beverage garnished with herbs from their garden. But, they emphasized, "You may not choose the herb. Rub the herb into your hands. Cup your hands. Breathe in. The herb must choose you."

Each guest was individually escorted to the herb garden. The intentionality, playfulness, and generosity were infectious. Beverages, herbs, great conversations, and, well, happiness flowed freely.

If happiness is not fully within our control, then we can at least give it the opportunity to more easily choose us.

Ecclesiastes 3:12-13

TRUSTING YOUR GOOD HEART

It can be difficult to trust God's heart, let alone your own. For you know what you think and feel some days, and much of it is not so good! As someone once said, "My thoughts can be a tough part of town."

Then there's Jeremiah, who declares, "The heart is more deceitful than all else, and is desperately sick."

But then the Cure came: Jesus. On the day you put your trust and hope in Jesus, you received a brand-new heart, brand-new spiritual DNA.

Don't worry about experiencing this immediately. God knows you need time and patience to mature. Your thinking will take some time to catch up with your new reality.

In the meantime, believing that your new heart is good and trustworthy will have a ripple effect on everyone and everything around you.

Here is the hard to believe truth: Christ lives in you. His heart has been fused with yours. Your new heart is good and trustworthy.

2 Corinthians 5:17

TRUSTING ANOTHER'S GOOD HEART

So you discover that you can begin to trust your heart because it has been made new. But what about others around you with new identities?

"Now wait just a minute. Trusting my heart is one thing, but his? Hers? Hold on! They seem to be wrong almost as often as they're right!" That's fair. Self-protection feels as natural as breathing. The only problem is that self-protection is an oxymoron.

Here's great news: God has been preparing you to receive His love practically and physically by trusting their good new heart. You don't have to trust everyone, or even anyone, right away. But trust is how you receive another's love, wisdom, insight, and protection.

They will still hurt you sometimes, but it's worth the risk to receive their love and protection. Once you experience that, it's a good gamble.

God has prepared those who love you deeply to care for you. Though they're not always right, God has made them to have so much that is right for you.

1 Thessalonians 5:11

5.3

FILLING THAT EMPTY PLACE

Blaise Pascal said, "There is a God-shaped vacuum in the heart of every man which cannot be filled by any created thing, but only by God."

The vacuum is not filled by assenting to a particular statement of faith—not by a more moral life, or political rightness; not by promises, or beating yourself up for doing wrong; not filled by what you stand against; not by formulas, techniques or patterns—and it is not filled by beating yourself up for not feeling filled!

It is filled by enjoying the Jesus who is over, above, under, through, within, amongst and within every molecule of your being. It is by trusting that Jesus really lives fused within you. You are filled in the comprehension that you are righteous, holy, beloved, enough, adored, forgiven, favored, and loved continually. God is not holding out until you get your act together. You can trust that out of the entire universe, He gives His full attention to you. These convictions allow you to give away His love.

Hebrews 2:5-8

WHEN TRUST GETS BROKEN

Deep sigh.

We've all experienced this from both sides. It can force us from open hands to the closed fists of self-protection.

God doesn't demand that you trust anyone. He knows trust is earned and that, when broken, coercion will not bring it back.

The heart trusts only when it knows it is safe to do so. This puts an onus upon the one who violated trust—but also upon the one violated. Although terrifying, for your sake, in time, you'll want to at least explore trusting again.

For if you learn to trust no one, then you will not be loved by anyone.

God invites you to forgive. First for your sake. This humility trusts God with the consequences and allows no hooks of bitterness or revenge. This is for you.

Then take a deep breath and trust that God is standing next to you as you risk going back out into a world capable of violating you. You know that only humility and trust will allow you to love and be loved well. There's no other way.

Ephesians 4:31-32

5.5

LOVE HAS A LANGUAGE

If love is primarily the process of meeting needs, then we can assume lovers search for the right words to get through to another's heart—"lovers" in the virtuous, compassionate, holistic meaning of lovers who are friends, colleagues, spouses, teammates, parents.

Their compliments contain no "catch," no partially veiled put-downs. Instead, refreshing encouragement is woven throughout even their critique. They are able to carry a significant role and title without lording it over anyone.

Their humor never belittles another. They are so trusted that even their back-and-forth banter is a clear demonstration of what safety looks like in a friendship.

They give the other the benefit of the doubt and are given the same— for nothing is more important to them than being able to win trust, affection, and permission. They display an unmanufactured playfulness that's kind, honest, and infectious. Others want in on it.

You sense it when you're around it. And once you've experienced it, you search for the language of lovers everywhere you go.

1 Corinthians 13:4-8

5.6

ADIRONDACK CHAIRS

Adirondack chairs weren't always this popular. Now front yard after front yard in neighborhoods across the land can have two or three chairs strategically placed on the front lawn. They come in a rainbow of colors.

But rarely does anyone seem to *sit* in the chairs! Maybe people are using them between the hours of 2 and 4 a.m. But it's doubtful. Homeowners appear to be saying, "We'd like to be people who sit in Adirondack chairs on our lawn. We'd like *you* to think we're the sort of folk who do. We're not. But we wish we were."

But you could break the Adirondack-chair wishful-thinking cycle. You could invite a friend or family member to come over and (gasp) sit in your chairs. You could talk about anything really—or even just be still for a while. Sitting in the chairs is the key. It is an intentional action on your part to create space for the truth "where two or three are gathered in My name."

There, sitting in your Adirondacks, God is present.

Acts 2:42,46-47

WHEN A CHILD IS SAD

Sadness is universal.

But deep-seated, lasting sadness, if not clinical, is a sign. We've either been hurt, have hurt someone, have not been loved well, or have experienced a significant unmet expectation. An adult can help locate and articulate the sadness. A child may only know they're sad.

A parent, trusted family friend, or teacher may be granted permission into the sadness. Galatians 6:2 teaches, "Bear one another's burdens, and thereby fulfill the law of Christ." You allow their burden to become yours. You explore reasons for their sadness. Mostly, they need you to convince them they won't face this alone.

You learn to teach them how to bring God into the center of their sadness. You give them dignity by explaining that they don't have to "get over it." With your help, they can be restored from any wrong they've done or that which was done to them. This is costly. But a child who has been loved well in sadness gets imprinted with health and a great sense of who they are.

Galatians 6:2

GRACE WHERE YOU WORK

Maybe you own or lead a business. You've discovered grace for your life, marriage, and friendships. But you've no idea how you'd implement it in your company. You're not even sure you'd want to. Profits are up. What would you do anyway? Make a campfire in the break room and sing Kumbaya?

Here's a starting point. Pick one person you work with closely. Go into their office and ask, "In my role, how am I affecting you?" They may stare at you like a deer in the headlights. Or they may give you an answer you don't like. Don't let either throw you. Stay with it. They must be convinced that you really want to know and that they'll not pay for their response. Over time, you can nurture an environment of grace with that person. Then start asking that question to others.

Trust has a ripple effect, possibly transforming the entire culture. Without giving up your authority, you're relationally leveling the playing field. In your vulnerability, protected by God, grace shows up at work.

Ephesians 6:9

CHOOSING A CAREER

"How can I be sure I will choose the right career?" This question is asked by many every day. And then there's a lament heard by many, decades into their career: "I chose the wrong path."

It all presumes there's only one exactly right career, and if you search hard enough you will invariably find it. Life is too complex for such simplicity. Values and interests mature; opportunities change.

But among those regretting career choices, a common refrain emerges from a lack of awareness: "I didn't know there was such a position. I would've loved doing that!" They're grieving their lack of exposure to a bigger world.

It's a lifetime gift for a parent or influencer to offer exposure to a wide range of opportunities. It's an equally big gift to dream with a young person about what life could look like. But it's most sacred of all to help a young person rest in the reality that God is guiding their journey to tap into who He has uniquely made them to be.

Ephesians 6:4

MORE THAN YOUR DESIRE FOR BACON

It's hard and wonderful to believe. At your core, more than anything else, you want to love well—more than satiating your desire for bacon, new shoes, or traveling to a foreign city.

But if it's true that the essence of Christ in you really *wants* to love God and others more than anything else, then life gets to be pretty great today. Go obey the new command, the one you can carry out, the one that doesn't cause you to rebel but causes you to want to do more of it. John 13:34 says, "A new commandment I give to you, that you love one another, even as I have loved you, that you also love one another."

It will get tested, and it won't feel like you will want to love others—especially the mean and grumpy ones. But eventually, it's what brings you the most satisfaction. You need nothing more today. Go, have a great life, one activity of love to another.

John 13:34

IN FRONT OF A FULL-LENGTH MIRROR

Beauty is a fascinating and complex concept. Paintings from centuries ago display an artist's conception of beauty that can bore or offend our current tastes and sensibilities. The same will probably one day be true with what future generations determine is beautiful.

So you wake up, look in the mirror, and nearly laugh or cry at what you see. There's little question that it's easier to admire a twenty-five-year-old face than an eighty-five-year-old face. It is perhaps also not as easy to look at yourself naked, out of the shower, after the scars of major surgery.

Your God is fully drawn to whom He sees in your mirror. He can perfectly pull all the factors into His equation of beauty. To Him, beauty involves His delight of you, the way He intentionally formed you, your courage, your trust, and His unchanging sensibilities. This is His definition of beauty. You are flat-out beautiful to the One who intentionally formed you.

Ephesians 5:25-27

5.12

A BEAUTIFUL SONG

Nobody told you when you became a Christian that you'd be thrown in with this bunch of characters from both sides of the aisle. They have such a strange language, idiosyncrasies, and musical tastes. You can seem like the only normal one in the faith. Eventually, you can feel like you don't belong.

What perhaps you cannot see is that God is assembling a Church from every political tribe and musical taste. It is part of what proves His supernatural choice of us. We are Barbarians, Scythians, vegetarians, gun owners, pacifists, Cretans, banjo players, mediators, meditators, addicts, libertarians, and hippies. We are Arabs, Persians, environmentalists, Civil War buffs, day traders, coal miners, merchant marines, zoologists, and federalists. As fervently as we may identify ourselves with them, none of these is our banner. We are fully "in Christ, vitally part of the body of Christ."

No community or group is nearly as diverse. God planned it this way. God is full of character.

Colossians 3:11

HEARTFELT OBEDIENCE AND ITS COUNTERFEIT

It is possible, from independent ability, to externally fulfill nearly everything God asks of you. And while it might look impressive to all, it is of little interest to God. He sees it's a ruse. He sees you pretending that you can somehow live this faith without dependence upon Him. You're pulling off the well-intentioned charade by compliance and not from the heart. All that work! Work without enjoying the relationship that would actually grow you.

Jesus is looking for the heartfelt response of men and women and girls and boys who enjoy letting His power play out through them. Romans calls it "obeying from the heart."

Anything less is man-made religion. Few things disgust Him more. It's a slap in the face of everything His Son accomplished. You can never get heartfelt obedience from anyone by perfecting such external religion. You'd be better off at the racetrack. But His grace has made it natural for you to "trust and obey."

Romans 12:9-10

5.14

OVER-OWNING STUFF

You can go through life with low-grade guilt concerning all the things you've never gotten around to. It can build to where you might feel the longing to step into a sensory-deprivation tank—for months.

Some of the angst may be accurate. When you broke up with your fiancé over text message? Yeah, you might want to make that right. Some angst has become time-expired. Like an email from nine years ago, asking you the name of a particular restaurant. They've moved on from it, and you can too.

If this inordinate guilt describes you, try this: Make two lists. One is all the things you have the capacity to do. Devise a strategy to implement them. The other list is all those things you know you will never do. For those, decide what alternate action needs to be taken, such as apologize, delegate, etc.

Everything else you don't have to own. Ever again.

Titus 2:14

DESTINY

You might wake up some days and think, *God, what am I supposed to do with my life? I'll work a career, maybe get married, and possibly buy a home with a gorgeous backyard. But why am I here?* Although it sounds like you're asking about potential, your question actually begs something much larger.

Destiny. The life journey God has sacredly prepared with your name on it.

Destiny is what happens when God-given desires mix with your particular giftings and are allowed to heal, mature, and release to be given away.

Does that stir your blood, at least a little? Although it may feel like a mystery, as you begin to trust God and others, your destiny will gradually come into focus. Ed Underwood encourages you to, "Live expectantly—God's signature on events is timing."

Although they don't yet know it, there are people waiting for you to show up in their stories. Your life is so very important. You could even look for some of them today. For destiny is not for someday. It's happening now.

1 Peter 2:9

5.16

WHEN LIFE GETS REAL

There can come a day when something causes you to lose confidence in your inborn capacity, moral superiority, natural bearing, or leadership qualities. Maybe you get hurt and can't figure out how to get unhurt. Or you fail in a way you never thought capable of. Or you get sick and lose some of the winsomeness and strength you led with. Maybe you've been bluffing about the health of your marriage. Maybe you realize your own kids have only been complying to your demands.

Many of those you've invested in have gone away, hurt you, or failed worse than before you got involved in their lives.

One day, perhaps you wake up and sigh, "God, I don't want to do this anymore. I've been a believer a long time. But I'm sorry. I feel like a phony."

Shortly after that moment, God gathers His angels, smiles, and says, "That right there. That was real. I'm going to be more able to inhabit this one's influence now."

Titus 3:3-6

GRACE IS NOT SRIRACHA

Grace makes some people nervous. Like it will lead us to not live wholly for God. Like it gives us permission to sin and just shrug our shoulders.

Such people see grace like a condiment, like sriracha, to be used only sparingly.

Or they're bound by that old cliche that grace must be balanced with something else. What? That's like saying you must balance your intake of air with something else.

All truth is in grace and all grace is in truth.

You don't need to fear grace.

Grace is not a condiment—nor the stuff of cliches. Think of grace as astonishingly good-tasting celery. You can have all you want and it'll only make you healthier.

Real grace does not free us to sin more. Grace actually defeats sin. Romans 6:14 says, "For sin shall not be master over you, for you are not under law but under grace."

Grace. Have all you want.

Romans 5:20-21

ENVIRONMENTS OF GRACE (PART ONE)

Grace isn't just a theology or a concept. It's an environment in which we choose to live. So what elements help form such a place? Well, among dozens of attributes, you'll always find these.

Relational commitments are prized above sanitized behavior. Authenticity and humility are essential. People still judge and gossip—they're immature after all—but leaders in these environments ensure that there is a process for helping people acknowledge how this affects others and for reconciling the people who have been compromised.

Forgiveness and repentance are ongoing ways of life. Listening comes before deciding. There's a measurably different consequence for telling on yourself than for being caught. You'll see empathy, caring, and kindness generously, yet imperfectly, displayed. Affirmation fills the air like confetti at a parade. Truth is cherished; each is learning how to best express it and hear it. You have more freedom to be yourself. Time together is essential. This life-giving place helps clarify your identity, enrich your gifts, and foster collective effectiveness.

Oh, and at the center of it all? Jesus.

Philippians 1:9

ENVIRONMENTS OF GRACE (PART TWO)

Regardless of where God places you, there is nothing more glorious or important to do with your life than to be part of a nurturing community of grace. Identity in Christ is taught routinely. It transforms our outlook on life to discover that the real us carries a shame-free identity and a core of actual righteousness and holiness. We listen to each other's stories. Superstars in this life discover that God and others here do not evaluate worth by stardom or celebrity. They honor one another in friendship. Those failing and facing consequences are also met with safety and restoration.

Strengths are submitted to and weaknesses are protected.

But this environment demands the sacrificial commitment of its leaders. There is a palpable, tangible sense of safety and acceptance the moment you enter into such a place, where leaders have put down roots. They've decided to stay for a full season, no matter how fragile or hurting the community becomes. This is real life others can sense and feel. This is grace. All are welcome.

Including you.

Ephesians 6:24

PROTECTION FROM THE ENEMY

". . . be on the alert with all perseverance and petition for all the saints" (Ephesians 6:18).

Everyone you know is in the crosshairs, fighting their fight: The ones who seem smug. The ones who bug you. The ones parading an arrogant life. The ones who seem to have it all together. Those estranged from you. Those who've hurt you. Those who say one thing and mean another. The critical and judgmental. The immature ones. Those who seem to have life by the tail. The callous. The indifferent ones.

Contrary to appearances, nobody gets a pass. We are all in a rarely abating struggle.

This is not a competition. We saints have an enemy, and we saints must pray for one another. That means even those described above. That doesn't necessarily mean reaching out with a hug. But it could mean remembering their names to our good Father: "Lord, help Travis. I know we're not the closest right now. But he is a fellow saint, a brother to me in You. Protect him, please. Amen."

Ephesians 6:18

5.21

WHY US?
(PART ONE)

We can imagine the room, that evening of Levi's invitation, the tax gatherer. It is full of actively immoral outcasts, carrying all manner of vile and visible scars of depravity, desperately trying to be on their best behavior. Quiet and awkward. If we could have filmed it, a camera would now pan in from the back of the room.

Soon there's a circle around Jesus, all of them with elbows on knees, chins on hands. Hardened sinners with sudden expressions of wonder. We're watching what happens when perfect love, authority, grace and purity invade darkness. The King has shown up to rescue prisoners from the enemy camp where wickedness, cynicism, and perversion have seemed logical up until this moment. Suddenly there is, at least in this room, a hope that life can be different.

The air gradually blends into a mixture of the stories, truth, life, and hope.

At some point in the evening, the conversation turns. "Who are You really?"

He's content to let the question linger in sacred silence. It is becoming clear exactly who He is.

Luke 5:27-32

5.22

WHY US?
(PART TWO)

Someone sitting next to Jesus quietly utters, "Why us? Why would You choose to be here tonight, with us?"

Jesus turns and kindly stares into the man's eyes a few seconds before answering: "This may be hard for you to understand. I've known and loved you since before there was time. I know about the catch in your knee that takes awhile each morning to loosen up. I was there the evenings your mother beat you. I was there when you were kicked out of the synagogue. I've come from heaven for you."

"But, do You know what I've done?"

"Yes, I know what you've done. And I have the troublesome ability to know the wrong things you're going to do tomorrow. The only sin that could possibly separate you from eternity with God is to reject the Person who's speaking with you at this very moment." Jesus smiles, "I'm really enjoying Myself tonight. It's so good to be here with you. All of you."

Luke 5:27-32

CONFUSING ANGER

Anger is not an inherently wrong emotion. Sometimes it's fitting and God-honoring. Like a valve, it opens in response to an injustice, and then it is meant to close. It's not supposed to stay open.

But some of us are angry 24/7—not toward anything or anyone in particular. We're just angry. We thought our new life in Christ would have solved things by now. We try to hide our anger from others. This just makes us angrier.

This can even happen to mature believers. Rejection, disappointment, failure—resentment builds up and they find themselves continually angry. Some carry a broken theology that keeps them in resentful comparison. Some feel helpless at news headlines, each day bringing something else to rage over.

If your anger valve feels always open, tell God about it. Coming clean about your anger can take away its irrational power.

Try this: Tell God two things you're really angry about and have no control over. Tell him any and all emotions. Pour out your anger. Now tell yourself this truth: God can handle hearing about what I can't possibly handle.

Ephesians 4:25-27

SHOCKING ANGER

Most of us can relate to "confusing" anger—that low-grade, ongoing anger at life. But we can also experience an irrational, sometimes violent, *over*-response to a particular situation. It shocks us.

"I could have done something really foolish just now, with serious consequences. My anger scares me sometimes. I could have seriously hurt someone. No one can know."

Most of us are subject to this darkness. Described in Galatians 5:20 as "outbursts of anger," it is an evidence of the flesh winning the moment.

Paul gives the long- and short-term remedy in Galatians 5:22-25 where "self-control," "patience," and "love" are presented as fruit of the Spirit. "If we live by the Spirit, let us also walk by the Spirit."

God is saying, "You are not a victim of your anger. That's not who you are. You no longer have to believe the real you will inevitably lose control. The Spirit within you is stronger. Count on My power in you. You will begin to see Me winning not just the hour but also the day."

Galatians 5:19-25

HOW TO EXPERIENCE LOVE

Many rarely experience love their entire lives. They mainly gain respect, admiration, even romantic attraction. But love, not so much. So what keeps them from experiencing love? It's largely this: None of us can experience another's love without trust. We involuntarily cannot let love in without a corresponding trust. Our ability to trust others determines how much love we'll enjoy on this planet.

The ability to trust comes from the humility to admit that we are not complete in ourselves. Others can give us what we simply do not possess and cannot create. God meets our needs. But He has chosen to not meet them exclusively while here on Earth. He's given us each other. This understanding of our need compels us to find those we can trust.

When our needs are met by a trustworthy other, we're experiencing love. Once we've risked it, we can't get enough of it.

Romans 12:4-5

GRACE—A WORKING DESCRIPTION

Grace is the absolute and unforced favor gained by Christ's death and resurrection, allowing God to be completely for us and endlessly in love with us, apart from anything we must prove. Grace is an actual reality, a way of life in which we no longer strive for acceptance. We mature, heal, and are released into His intentions by trusting that all the power of Jesus is fused in us, creating an entirely new person.

We get to take these words and let them wash over the landscape of our lives. We get to imagine life if we let go of the paltry religious "ought" many of us ground out for so long. We get to sit with our friends and dream together about what this would mean to our relationships, our communities, our churches, our nations. We get to sit by the shore and laugh to ourselves that such a life has found such as us.

2 Peter 3:17-18

GRACE—
AN ETERNAL
DESCRIPTION

Grace began with the Trinity. It was not invented to address sin. Grace is how Jesus, the Father, and the Holy Spirit have always interacted and loved each other. It's the only way God wants to interact with and love us.

Grace is God's primary gift to us—the means to our salvation, the basis for our maturing. Grace is the key to relationships of love, the foundation for our communities, and the doorway to our destinies.

When trusted, we learn love, learn ourselves, and see the true face of God. Grace is the experience of all Christ's unmerited favor from His payment on the cross. Grace is not in competition with truth or justice. Grace is not a six-week series or merely a theological concept to balance against another. Grace is an environment, a power, and a life course. It's the air we breathe.

Breathe deeply.

John 1:16-18

5.28

DR. ROSSCUP

It's not easy to know whether this story about Dr. Rosscup is true or not. But knowing the New Testament seminary professor even a little persuades you to want to believe it happened.

A student called Dr. Rosscup to explain his dilemma: "I've been busy in ministry and am taking a full load in seminary. Last weekend I moved from one apartment to another. Then my wife got sick. Your final paper is due tomorrow. I know you said there were no exceptions. But I can't do it in time. I'm asking you for a one-day extension."

"I cannot do that. For twenty years students have had to come under the same requirements as you."

"But please. I'll fail and I already have a church waiting for me to graduate."

"I cannot make an exception for you. Justice will not allow it." Then the line got quiet for a few moments. "But if you'll allow me, I'll finish writing your paper for you."

Please, God. Allow this story to be true.

Romans 5:1-9

GOD'S YOUR FRIEND

Trusting your new identity in Christ accentuates a breathtaking treasure: Jesus is your Friend. You take Christ and the awesome Holy Spirit with you everywhere you go!

They love you. And, have all kinds of incredible things to share with you. So keep your eyes wide open and your ears tuned to what they may have to share with you during the moments of your day. They will point out truth to you, show you people to care for, and invite you to do "impossible" things. Conversations with God brim with promises, ideas, and joys. Both in your solitude and on-the-go. This is what the flourishing biblical encouragement means: "Let your prayer be constantly recurring."

True, sometimes you need to check with your trusted friends what you think you are hearing from God. We've known people who were sure God told them they should marry a certain person, only to later discover that person was already married. Oops.

Meanwhile, every week, you and God have amazing things to discuss. Don't miss the wonder of it all.

1 Thessalonians 5:17

HELLO AGAIN

Hi. As God it's important for Me to tell you that today I will be with you in everything you face. You will experience no problem or enjoyment alone. In any moment that feels scary or overwhelming, just stop for a moment and realize I am right here with you. In any moment that feels magnificent or breathtakingly funny, I'm right here with you.

How can I do this for you *and* everyone else? You don't have to worry about that; just trust Me. I simply want you to know that I do it completely and individually for *you*. Every day.

I've noticed that some days you forget My presence in those overwhelmingly stressful times. You don't need to do anything to make up for that. I get it. I just want you to know that I'm as here as anyone you see today. In some ways I'm here even more—because I care about you more than you care about you. So, here we go. Enjoy My presence. I sure do enjoy yours.

Matthew 14:22-33

"Jesus set us free so that we could live in a new and different reality."

-Lay it Down

JUNE

JUNE

JUNE

JUNE

JUNE

JUNE

@truefacelife

@truefacecommunity

WHEN YOU DON'T FEEL LIKE TALKING TO GOD

Many of us learned to pray as an obligation, largely as a way to keep God good with us. Then one day, maybe, we discovered He *is* good with us. And we began to talk to Him when we wanted to, instead of when we felt we "had to."

You'll probably have moments like, "Hey, wait! I haven't talked to Him for a while. What's wrong with me? I wonder if He's disappointed with me."

And you may be tempted to run back to how it was before, back before you knew you were free. It may feel safer, but it's not.

Before you run, remember two things: (1) He lives in you and wants you to experience your freedom; and (2) He's not resentful when you miss time with Him. Nothing delights Him more than you *wanting* to talk, not feeling like you have to.

Psalm 42

TREASURES FROM GOD

Every morning you wake up, something marvelous has been laid out while you were sleeping. Paul describes it like this: "Good works which God prepared beforehand so that we would walk in them."

Imagine that! Great things He has for you to do. Specifically designed for your gifting, maturity, and capacity. For you to stumble upon as you walk through your day.

Treasures, with your name on them! Sometimes they are not obvious. You may miss a few. Relax. He knows how to bring them back again another day.

Isn't that life-giving?

"Good works" usually involve sacrifice. Grace is not opposed to effort. Grace is opposed to effort for the wrong reasons. So, enjoy what you've been wanting to do all along: meaningful, important, valuable works of love. The new you reverberates with a desire to serve. Take a look around your life today. You'll be surprised at how many "works" you're already walking in.

Ephesians 2:10

OUR DEAR GOD

We try to hide this from You. It sounds absurd even saying that.

Some of us were sexually abused.

It messed us up. Some for much of our lives. Even though we've been told we shouldn't, we feel ashamed, guilty, dirty, second-class. We've prayed it would go away. It doesn't. We carry it into every social setting: this relentless voice hissing that we will always be damaged and unclean. We've tried to forgive ourselves for our part. But we're not even honestly sure what our part was. It's all hazy. That's what abuse does. It stains everything dark.

You say in Hebrews 12:2 that You did something with our shame at the cross. You actually experienced it and bore its shamefulness. You claim You broke the power of sin and shame in us and replaced it with a clean, Jesus-infused identity. Could we, the shamed ones, really believe that? Would it free us? Oh, please, let it be. Thank You, dear Jesus.

Isaiah 61:7

TOO OLD TO GO BACK

One of the most liberating moments in life is when you discover that the real you doesn't want to get away with anything. Your motives are not dishonorable. That ship sailed at the cross. You're a new creature: Christ in you. You're fused together with Him. Loved beyond all telling by a God who never makes a mistake and who will eventually refashion any misfortune, in some manner, into something that can bring you good.

You're not looking for a loophole. Loved completely, forgiven always, enjoyed without end, changed already—you are free to not stress over who you might think you should be by now. And you won't trade any of that in for the illusion of stability in self-effort, striving, performing or complying. No matter what age you are, you are too old to go back to prison.

Galatians 3:3

DISCOVERING YOU HURT A FRIEND

It's hard to admit. Yes, once again, you hurt someone you care about. It's embarrassing. And you fear if you admit to it, you'll set back their trust indefinitely. You may be tempted to rationalize, justify, or put the blame onto the other. Even if they've done wrong, your part is to own the hurt you have caused.

God gives a great gift to free your heart and help free theirs: *repentance*. He gives you a heart of humility stronger than your fear of exposure. Before you talk to your friend, talk to God and admit what you did. Count on what Jesus did at the cross to free you and help you feel truly clean. Now you're ready to go to your friend.

You ask them to express what you did and how it affected them. You tell them specifically what you heard and that you believe them. You ask for forgiveness, willing to make right what is wrong.

Don't be surprised if their trust of you increases instead of diminishes. Redemption is that powerful.

2 Corinthians 7:10

SHARING GRACE (PART ONE)

When grace grabs hold of us, at least two responses quickly follow. First, "Where has this truth been all of my life?" We don't always ask this with great joy. It's deeply disappointing to discover that these truths have been here all of our lives but were not taught or modeled by those who mentored us.

The second response is to tell everyone we know about this grace. They will, of course, respond with the same excitement and world-view shift as we did. Right? Well, sometimes it works like that. Most often it does not. We forget how long it took us to receive this grace. Others may have been trying to teach us. We weren't ready. Most of us have a tightly conceived theology that doesn't often get dismantled in a week.

Grace cannot be coerced. It's a transaction between God and a human. That's right, the reception of grace is a supernatural transaction. None of this will curb your passion. Nothing should. But it might at least calm your expectations.

Ephesians 3:6-10

SHARING GRACE (PART TWO)

It may take awhile for your friends and family to embrace the grace you've been embracing. But it's encouraging to know that many have been privately hoping this is how God is and how He has ordered His world. They just weren't certain anyone believed it. Apart from justification by grace, sanctification by grace may be the very best news we ever receive.

When you're given the privilege to be the messenger who explains it, some will carry a bond of gratefulness for you that will remain the rest of their lives. In the same way that some can remember the day and the hour they put their hope in Jesus Christ, so too some can remember the exact moment living by grace made sense. So, while not everyone's poised to receive this message of life immediately, some just need to hear that someone else believes it (that'd be you) and that grace is what the Word of God has been truly teaching all along. Be prepared to receive gratitude for the rest of your life!

Romans 10:15-17

THE PERFECT LIFE

It's easy to watch movies, social media, or the family next door and feel like your life is *less than*. For example, you may be single or divorced, watching married couples in a restaurant with their kids, laughing and playing. It's easy to presume they've got it made, that their life is perfect.

But if you could watch a highlight, or maybe more accurately, a lowlight reel of their lives, you'd discover that they carry the same pain, confusion, disappointment, and failure as you do. It may look a little different, but it's the same.

There will probably always be those more mature, healthier, and more balanced than you. But God has given you, within whatever limitations you carry, the ability to enjoy your life as much as anyone else. There are no perfect people. There is no perfect life. There is us. And there is God who loves us. We're invited to trust Him with the gift of our lives. Joy is the result. It doesn't get much better than that.

Psalm 139:23-24

WORK IS A GIFT (PART ONE)

Most of us see work as a necessary evil. It pays the bills. It allows us to finance braces, college loans, or maybe a timeshare in Tahiti. But most of us say we'd quit if we won the lottery.

But the stats say lottery winners are no happier than the rest of us. Seriously.

We were designed to work, even to enjoy it. God knew we needed purpose and a sense of accomplishment that couldn't come from recreation alone. Work is a gift from God. To apply ourselves in it deeply is ultimately as satisfying and needed as any vacation.

Work can be quite physical, like clearing your backyard of kudzu. Or it can be primarily mental, such as helping a friend solve a financial problem. Then again, it could be both, for example helping a friend remodel a bathroom.

God has satisfying work waiting to be done by you. He has friends and colleagues to help you explore what work would be most profitable and meaningful to your heart.

Ecclesiastes 9:10

WORK IS A GIFT (PART TWO)

If we agree that work is a gift from God, then the trick appears to be finding meaningful and life-giving work. For some, that can seem a continual challenge. We all know people who regret choices they made early on. For many it is too difficult or costly to change their career mid-stream. Many endure long years in a job they resent.

It doesn't have to play out this way.

At any stage, it is invaluable to discover a mature friend, mentor, or employer who watches your life, interests, and curiosity. They may have creative ideas and connections to do something like shadow someone for a day whose job you vicariously enjoy. They can reveal fields matching your passion and competency you may not know about. These people often ask insightful questions and can expose you to a variety of vocations and career settings. Of course, the key in all of this is to pay attention, to be open, and to stay curious as to what these valuable people have to say about our lives and the good work we might do.

Ecclesiastes 9:7

WHERE CHOICES FIND A FOREVER HOME

Somewhere on this planet, in this moment, someone is engaged in conversation about Jesus with one who does not yet know Him. We all know too many embarrassing, destructive examples of such inter-actions. This is not one of them. This one is full of grace, vulnerability, and respect.

Maybe they are friends. Many times faith is not discussed at all. Instead, their talk leans to beverages, clothing, movies, funerals, and broken hearts. There has been no catch, no agenda, no formula. You'd be so proud of the way this person is representing your God. You might be equally proud of the friend.

Now, in this moment, maybe God is allowing those words about the cross, the resurrection, about love and salvation to finally make sense. It would be a fine thing to call out to God to thank Him for what He's doing and to thank Him for those friends—for they sure-ly exist, somewhere. One day you will meet them both, in the land where such choices find a forever home.

2 Corinthians 5:20-21

YOU PROBABLY CAN'T SPEED IT UP (PART ONE)

How can you describe playful, God-centered freedom? Maybe you can't. You only know you stumbled into it. Now it's the reason you're fairly sure you'll make it through the storms. For a while, you were anything but playful. You were the most sold-out, diligent, religious human most had met. And you were miserable. Few are more miserable than a religiously miserable person.

Now you still get sad, confused, even bewildered. But you're done with that miserable mess. It's what you're slowly beginning to become convinced of that's transforming you: God is absolutely delighted with you.

You can't speed up believing in complete acceptance. You can't speed up believing you're adored. You can't speed up believing you're not behind. You can't speed up believing you're enough. You can't speed up letting go of trying to maintain your good Christian testimony. You can't speed up not listening to shame voices. You can't speed up believing you can just relax and enjoy and love whatever God puts in front of you. But when it begins to happen, shame runs off the stage.

Galatians 5:18-26

YOU PROBABLY CAN'T SPEED IT UP (PART TWO)

So much has changed since you began to believe you are who God says you are. Pain is still pain. Glare is still glare. Loss is still gut-wrenching. *But you're free*. So you play differently. You dream differently. You love differently. You relax differently. You affirm and bless. You receive. You love non-Christians instead of pitying them—or envying them. You believe the world will change not by desperately trying to fix it but by loving it.

It means drawing closer to those who fail and allowing others to draw close when you fail. It means risking love and being willing to be fooled. It means giving up an agenda for others' lives. It means believing we have new hearts, and therefore giving our motives the benefit of the doubt. It means needing to impress no one and yet finding great joy in pleasing many. It means allowing Jesus to correct you, without hearing a voice of displeasure. You can't speed this up, but when you begin to believe it, your new life gets a chance to thrive.

1 Peter 2:16

PLOTTING JOY

One of the grand benefits of having a heart that most wants to love is that you get to love. At any time of any day, you can start plotting what would bring joy to another. It can be simple or elaborate. You can pull it off right away or months from now—for your kids or the guy at the office who mocks your footwear.

It could be hiding to watch a spouses' reaction as you go beyond expectations on a project they've been nagging you to do. You can stun that guy in the office by secretly leaving a box of favorite doughnuts on his desk with a note sharing what the team enjoys about him. It could be plotting with others an overnight getaway for your spouse, while you scheme an evening for your kids that uniquely fits their joy. Look at that, two plottings in one!

Bring God in on it. Talk about it with Him. He enjoys plotting joy a lot. He's been doing it for you all your life.

John 17:13-23

A GOOD FATHER AT LAST

God as the good Father. How do you embrace that when your earthly father was not? Or is not? God as the good Father, for some of us, is like a dream we're convinced will never come true.

Yet there is in all of us this innate capacity to believe and receive a truly wonderful Father, even if we didn't have one growing up. So how do you begin to let an invisible God be the good father you never had?

Baby steps, that's how.

It starts as you tell Him how hard it has been to live without a good father. You ask Him to reveal Himself in your hour-to-hour life. You allow His commitment to replace the lies you believed because your father did not love you well. You choose to risk believing that God the Father never forgets appointments or makes time for something other than you.

This doesn't happen overnight. Daring to believe God as the good Father you never knew is a supernatural transaction. Remember: baby steps.

Psalm 68:5

SOMEONE THEY CAN TRUST

There is no greater gift you can give your child than to be someone they can trust.

No greater gift? That's quite a statement. But think about it a minute. Children arrive here like trust-sponges, just looking for someone to trust so they can grow up safe and secure, with a sense of significance. Sadly, many never find that someone. Now some don't even know they've missed it. They simply feel fearful, angry, resentful and cynical, and they aren't sure why.

What about you? As a child, did you have someone you could trust? A parent? A grandparent? Maybe even a schoolteacher? Take a minute and push back into your memories. Try to remember what it was about that person that you found trustworthy.

And in a very real sense, we're all children. So, how could you show yourself trustworthy today?

2 Timothy 3:10

LOVE IS NOT

Love is not passion, attraction, or what most love songs claim it to be.

Love is not about getting something to make your life work. Love is not clutching or possessing. It is never revocable. Love does not cease to exist when it is discarded. Love is not merely emotion or poetic words on a page. Love is not fantasy. Love is not rekindling a memory of one who is no longer yours. Love is not attempting to change another to become like you.

Love is not appeasing to keep peace or ignoring to avoid conflict. Love is not static, guaranteed to stay warm. Love is not an energy a couple creates. Love is not repeatable by revisiting where you once knew it. Love is not manufactured by setting, location, or any human.

It is given as a gift by a God who names Himself Love.

1 John 4:7-9

LOVE IS

Love champions another. Love stays, almost embarrassingly, after all others have left.

Love earns a way in to be trusted, to enter a wound or a limitation. Love pulls closer when another fails. Love stands against what threatens to harm. Love is trustworthy when another finally trusts you with their worst. Love gives the benefit of the doubt, when there is plenty to doubt. Love gives plenty of room to fail.

Love stands boldly next to the outcast. Love is willing to sit on a stoop with the infectiously sick, risking to contract their disease. Love is able to make laughter safe. Love is able to handle sin. Love alone is able to do that. Love takes the hit.

Love is willing to give up being right in order to do right. Love is impossible to do independently. Love is what God has chosen to reveal in you.

1 Corinthians 13

INDIANA HOTEL (PART ONE)

You might be reading this alone in a hotel room, on the road, far from home. Like maybe in Indiana. Indiana feels far from home even if you're from Indiana.

It's late. You've lost interest in your phone apps and cable news. You're suddenly overwhelmed with a familiar sexual enticement. You are usually prepared. This time, you aren't. Maybe something earlier in the day set this moment in motion.

But now, in desperation, you've opened the book to this page. You're already feeling shame and haven't done anything—yet. But you know you probably will.

So do this. You have friends back home you trust. Dial until one of them answers. Tell the person the failure you are intending to commit. It will help break the chain. Sin wields its power in hiddenness and darkness.

And there it is. Friendship. Now make that call.

Galatians 6:1-2

INDIANA HOTEL (PART TWO)

You're still alone in that hotel room, on the road, far from home. Let's say it's even later. You chose to call no one. And you acted out.

You tried to resist this attack. But you had no chance to defeat this once it started. You were trying to resist something you'd already given yourself permission to do. Now you are in the aftermath of a reality you cannot unwind.

For this cycle is not done yet. You know the drill. If you stay private with this, you will beat yourself up for a while. Then you will withdraw, rationalize, and blame someone or something else. Then you'll heap another layer of shame onto the story you tell yourself about you. It will leave you washed up on the shore of cynical disillusionment.

But even now, you can stop the madness. A phone call will stop the cycle. You cannot undo what has been done. But you can stop *this* in its tracks.

Make the call.

Romans 4:7-8

INDIANA HOTEL (PART THREE)

Still alone in that hotel room, on the road, far from home.

Let's say it's now 12:40 a.m. You still can't sleep. You called a friend. It went so much better than you could have hoped. You felt known, protected and loved. But you still feel dirty. Like Macbeth, you discover you can't wash this evening away.

The gospel is not just good news for some day far off. The gospel is for now. Jesus accomplished the ability to cleanse you in this very moment! No matter what you've done, you can feel clean again. Now. Jesus is that real and that powerful!

Repentance is not a promise from you to Him; it is a gift from Him to you. It's moving from your independent insufficiency to His ability in you. Repentance is asking His shed blood to restore innocence to your heart's experience—the Innocent One surging a renewed innocence through you.

You don't have to grovel or do penance. Just trust in His ability to make you clean.

Now do try to get some sleep, friend. You've been through a lot.

Psalm 51

THE LAST TO KNOW

Driven people can be the most susceptible to the Law. With the Law you at least know where you stand. You do nine things right, you get credit for nine. Maybe you're only checking boxes, but checking things off is satisfying!

God is concerned both with your heart and the behavior. So when you discover, after say a decade or two, that you can still be pretty judgmental and unloving toward others, what do you do with that? Did grace not take? Is God choosing to not work through you? Did you mess up the paperwork?

It is not uncommon to miss or ignore the maturity that is happening in us. You might not give yourself credit for the good, while being hyper-vigilantly aware of the bad. You assume that without 100% improvement it must mean that there is no improvement.

This is why clarity from your trusted friends is so important. They see you and your wins more accurately than you can. God hasn't forgotten to work through you. He just takes the long view. Don't worry.

Sometimes you're just the last to know.

Philippians 3:12-16

A MOMENTARY
SABBATH REST

All of it has a certain rhythm, an almost eternal familiarity. That place in the day that is yours alone. The way you prepare your coffee or tea. The magnified sounds of a pattern you've created. Almost always nearly the same. The route around the kitchen island. The glow of an antique lamp. The particular texture of your favorite chair. It's as though these objects have awaited your return. Because it is so consistent, you don't have to think about it. You're free to muse the day, to reflect on how you feel, what's nagging at you, what's bringing you joy, what you might adapt to or change.

There are few such resting places in the day for most of us.

God inhabits this sanctuary also. He enjoys the pattern, the order, the routine. He helped you form it. He knows it's essential for your health and heart. So, today, enjoy that place of rest in the routine. He's enjoying it with you. He is a good Father.

Hebrews 4:9-10

LETTING THE CLEAR INTERPRET THE UNCLEAR

If you come to the scriptures anticipating condemnation, you'll find it.

Matthew 6:15 seems to show that our forgiveness is conditional: "But if you refuse to forgive others, your Father will not forgive your sins." It's like the Father is saying, "Hey, I noticed you didn't forgive that person. So, I'm afraid I'm going to have to change My mind and not forgive you." Ouch.

A helpful interpretive principle is to let the *clear interpret the unclear.* Romans 5–8, Ephesians 1, and a significant body of clear scripture teach that we're justified and forgiven, unconditionally accepted—period. So, we let those scriptures inform us to interpret this one.

Jesus is talking about experiential forgiveness, not judicial forgiveness. While justified once and for all, we may not experience the beauty of that forgiveness if we don't forgive others. He's saying, "I'm encouraging you to forgive this person. I want to heal, restore, and begin freeing you from this trauma. You must allow the cross to cleanse you of this so that you can experience the forgiveness I've already given."

Romans 5–8

CONTEXT, CONTEXT

Trusting your identity is no small thing. It defines how you'll read Romans and whether you'll live in peace or fear. Romans 8 describes those "in the Spirit" and those "in the flesh." If you see the descriptions as degrees of a believer's obedience, then you'll strive to be more "in the Spirit" to escape the "death" promised to those "in the flesh."

Romans 8:5-6 says, "For those who are according to the flesh set their minds on the things of the flesh, but those who are according to the Spirit, the things of the Spirit. For the mind set on the flesh is death, but the mind set on the Spirit is life and peace."

The context is so important here. Romans 8:9 says, "However, you are not in the flesh but in the Spirit." Paul is writing to people who aren't in the flesh but in the Spirit. It's not a to-do-list. It's stating a *fact* that is already true about you.

It's a description of you, not an assignment for you.

Romans 8:1-11

CHECK-IN TIME

The end of the day is a great time to check in—with a friend, spouse, children, parents or colleagues. It doesn't necessarily need to be profound. It's simply giving dignity to each other's day on this planet. There are dozens of questions you could ask. Here are a few: "What overwhelmed you today?" "What made you happiest?" "Did anyone hurt your heart?" "What did you learn that you can't wait to tell me?"

Find a comfortable place and just start. It may drag and devolve awkwardly at times. But you're together, giving dignity. Eventually a five-minute check-in can be the anticipated setting where you get to tell on yourself. It can change the quality of your relationships. It's suddenly possible to tell things you're struggling with and have others able to enter in with you. So many good things, all because you took the risk to be intentional.

Fight hard for that check-in time. It will become one of the safest, strongest places in your life.

Acts 2:46-47

OWNING YOUR INFLUENCE (PART ONE)

Who gives you permission to influence their life? It's a sobering and vitally important question to ask. That person has watched you for some time and, in some measure, has chosen to trust your influence upon their life. They're saying, in essence, "I'm counting on you to be a good person. God has allowed you to earn a way into my life. I've bought in to who you are—how you see life, how you do life. I usually take your words as counsel, not just opinion or advice. Often, if it disagrees with my own, I'm tempted to trust your assessment. I respect you. I know you're mortal and flawed like the rest of us. I don't agree with all your politics. I realize you could let me down. But you are mature and good. I'm listening carefully to you even when we're just hanging out."

You've been given an incredible gift. Owning your influence means, from that moment forward, to love them, counsel them, and commit to see their influence released.

1 Timothy 1:1-4

OWNING YOUR INFLUENCE (PART TWO)

So, another person has chosen to trust you to help influence their lives.

It's one of the great privileges this life affords. You get to take it seriously. They are trusting you with them. They are letting you in. They're allowing you to meet needs they cannot. So talk about what influence means to you. Ask what it means to them.

If they tell you they trust you with everything, tell them not to. Let them know what you can and cannot be trusted to protect them in. Commit to draw close in the areas you know you can love them well. You don't have the same freedoms you did before someone chose to let you love them. Careless inconsistency will confuse them. Simply be yourself, that's all. You will fail. You will fail them. If you own your failure, they're built to forgive you, with little or no loss of faith.

God has given you a sacred trust. Christ in you is getting to love, protect, and help another human flourish.

2 Thessalonians 3:7-9

OWNING YOUR INFLUENCE (PART THREE)

There's a universe of difference between *influence* and *control*. A controller wants to fix your issues. An influencing friend cares more about fostering an open environment of trust. The influencer convinces you of your actual righteousness. The controller measures your righteousness by how little you sin. The influencer is more concerned about how you're giving and receiving love. They know that sinning less will not help you love more but that loving more will allow you to sin less.

A controller makes you morally accountable so that they can control your behavior, which will only make you hide more. An influencing friend earns permission to protect you. You hide less in the safety of their commitment. Unresolved issues emerge into the light for healing.

Controllers have lost confidence in the power of God's grace, fearing it will keep you from taking sin seriously enough. The influencer wants you to believe only grace is strong enough to deal with sin.

Think about who you allow to influence you. Consider if there's anyone trying to control you. Remember, there's a big difference here.

Galatians 5:13-14

HALFWAY

So, we're halfway through this year, and this book. At this point, it might be good to consider several questions. First, how has this book affected the way you see life on a daily basis? By now you realize we're presenting a way of seeing. We are presenting how grace hopefully looks from dozens of vantage points. So, again, is this book changing how you see your daily life?

Second, how is this book affecting your relationships? Are you using these stories and thoughts to engage with others? Some of you may be reading this book only because you promised your parents you would. We'll take any motive—even if you're reading it because you lost a bet. But we're hoping you are deeply engaging with these daily reminders of how God sees you and how you can see Him, yourself, and others. Please take some time with these questions. We wish we could be with you to listen in.

We've saved some of our favorite pieces for the second half. Enjoy.

Psalm 127:1

"Will we accept only that which we can accomplish on our own? Or will we begin to climb the character ladder, trusting God to lead us to a destiny far greater than we can imagine?"

-Ascent of a Leader

JULY

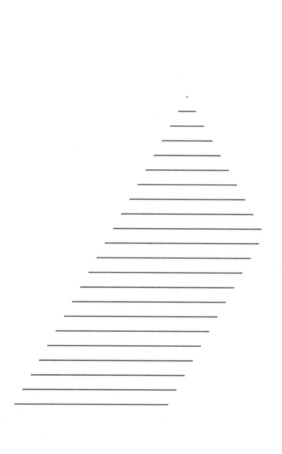

BAD WATER

Fresh water enriches and replenishes just about everything in your body. There's nothing like it on the whole planet! But drink polluted water and you might live with amoebas, dysentery, diarrhea, and, ironically, dehydration and thirst!

True in the physical realm. True in the spiritual realm.

Most Christians trust the Original Water for saving *but not for living*. They first drank from the Headwaters, but they've wandered downstream into contaminated waters. Now they're working hard, drinking more polluted water, faster, to overcome their sickness.

"Authentic" means to be "uncorrupted from the original." The route to authenticity is clear: You must get back to the Headwaters.

When you drink corrupted water, you live sick. You start to trade freedom for bondage, joy for drudgery, relaxation for compulsiveness, compassion for criticism, peace for anger, love for sin, friendship for alienation, vision for myopia, finishing well for flaming out.

Jesus said, "Whoever drinks of the water I will give him will never be thirsty again."

You've got to get back.

John 4:14

ACROSS THE AISLE

It can be hard to imagine grace invading the polarized division between parties in Washington, DC.

Enter Tony Hall. While a Democratic member of the House of Representatives, Hall was nominated for the Nobel Peace Prize *three times*. For many decades he's been a leading advocate for hunger relief programs throughout the world.

What's less known is the world-changing friendship between Hall and *Republican* Frank Wolf. In 1984, the two were second-term congress members. Both Christians, they met together for prayer and Bible study. One day Hall risked asking Wolf to take a trip to Ethiopia to witness the effects of the famine: "I won't be able to help them unless I have a partner, and I need you." Over the next thirty years, their trust in each other allowed them to tackle issues facing the poor and vulnerable. Their shared trust from their love of Jesus allowed them to stand shoulder to shoulder in defense of others.

God might want to do something meaningful with you and a friend you disagree with on many things.

Colossians 3:10-11

WHEN YOU AREN'T BRAVE

There will be times, no matter how long or well you've trusted God, that you won't respond with bravery.

You'll stand in frozen indecision as someone else rushes into the situation to offer the Heimlich maneuver. You'll be tempted to feel ashamed. You failed a test you won't get to retake.

Your life in Christ looks like this. There will be days when you shock yourself in heroic poise, and there will be days when you shock yourself in petty self-interest.

Same person. Same faith.

Abraham, the father of the New Covenant, told Abimelech that Sarah was his sister to avoid personal danger. David, God's own friend, sent Uriah to be killed in battle to cover his tracks. Barnabas and Paul parted ways for some time over a conflict they couldn't work out.

There are no unwaveringly brave people. There are only new creatures imprecisely maturing into who they already are under His delighted eye.

Unwavering God. Unwavering love.

John 21:15-17

COACH BERGMAN

He wore a plain felt ball cap, a white tucked-in T-shirt, and dress slacks cinched up high. He chewed on a cigar stub he never lit. He talked to people through it. None of the players' parents seemed to care. Coach Bergman was allowed to coach Elks League teams at Coronado Park in Phoenix for forty summers.

One player had never been on a 60-foot, 6-inch mound before Bergman told him, "Kid, you're pitching Tuesday night. I watched how you warmed up. You can do it." In his second outing, the kid threw a no-hitter. Most of Bergman's players would say he was the best coach they ever had.

To the early church, Barnabas was their Coach Bergman, minus the cigar (see Acts 4:36). Barnabas convinced them they mattered, and he wouldn't quit on them for making mistakes.

God does that for us, and He has lodged this quality of grace—discerning encouragement—in all of us. It's a joy in this life to slow down long enough to *see* others so we can help them flourish.

Proverbs 2:6-11

FEELING UNAPPRECIATED

The motivation for acts of love comes from Christ in us. But, heck, we still carry unspoken expectations that they'll show us appreciation in return. Not everyone. Just those important to us.

Occasionally, everything conspires against you. You get left out, snubbed, or overlooked. Others get credit for something you did (the evil one knows your exact susceptibilities). One day, worn out from doing good, you find yourself feeling bitterly unappreciated. From that moment, it twists into feeling unloved.

This can be stopped in its tracks as you allow another in. God uses other people to protect and reorient our hearts. You verbalize it. Even if you feel ashamed, your trusted friends rarely will. Letting them hear the truth, and any untruths, allows sweet magic to happen. The cycle of victimization can stop. You can then accurately grieve being overlooked, while no longer turning it into more.

The next time you feel under-appreciated, tell a friend, "I'm feeling discouraged and could use a reminder of the good work God is doing in and through me."

2 Thessalonians 3:13

WHAT CAN'T BE TAKEN

If you've been on a flight anytime in the recent past, you've heard a voice declare, "Please do not congregate in the aisles or near the bathroom. Thank you." It makes you wonder what will be next. "Please, do not scratch your scalp or adjust your socks in the main cabin area. Thank you."

Almost everywhere, our personal freedoms are being curtailed by the actions of some with ill-intent or those with limited common sense. It probably won't improve anytime soon.

But what cannot be curtailed or legislated are the conversations you have in prayer. A lavish world of unrestricted freedom and wonder is spread in front of you—a God who doesn't need to protect Himself from insurance risk, terrorists, lawyers, or "acts of God." He listens as though you were the only human on the planet. He has endless time to talk about and dream about everything and nothing.

Go. Enjoy. You may congregate, wander around, and sit in His first-class cabin. He said so.

Jude 1:20

HELLO AGAIN

Hi. It's Me, your God.

Today I wanted to simply share something fun and amazing that you might not have considered. My child, I live simultaneously outside and inside of time. I see up ahead in your story. So I get to enjoy your exciting, exhilarating, heroic, and amusing moments before you step into them. I get to drink their goodness in more than once. You have the experience itself and the memory of it. I get to experience the event, carry the memory of it, and experience the event *before* it happens. Pretty cool, huh?

Anyway, I just wanted you to know that there are some supremely good moments up ahead.

That's all. I love you.

Romans 11:33-36

SAVORING LIFE

A great indication you are trusting the grace of God is being able to savor your life. If you're not convinced of His favor, grace, and love, then no amount of working seems enough and any amount of relaxation can seem too much.

In Ecclesiastes 9:7, Solomon says, "Go then, eat your bread in happiness and drink your wine with a cheerful heart; for God has already approved your works." You're approved by God, so go, eat, drink, and celebrate in happiness! No one gets to be your judge, including you. You'll overdo on either side at times. But God's not keeping score. He knows your heart.

You are a new creature with a new heart that can be increasingly trusted. You don't want to take advantage of God. You've already decided your life belongs to Him. You work as a trusted friend, not a hired hand. You've discovered He's not a harsh master but a gracious host who sits down to enjoy Himself right in the middle of your celebration. Cheers!

2 Timothy 2:1

SELF-CARE

"I have come to believe that caring for myself is not self indulgent. Caring for myself is an act of survival." –*Audre Lorde*

Audre is describing a behavior and attitude infinitely and qualitatively different from self-indulgence. Self-indulgence tries to fill what feels withheld and owed. Self-indulgence comes from believing I am not worth truly being cared for by God. So I create my own self-protective choices of excess or immorality, fighting to get enough to be finally satisfied.

Self-care describes the choice of one convinced they're inhabited by the very God of the universe. It is the admission that I am not a marginally tolerated sinner but a constantly adored new creature, carrying the very nature of God Himself. I realize time is not mine to fritter away by filling it with tension, work, or spartan-like self-denial.

Self-care is an intentional choice of goodness—for God, for those we love, and yes, for ourselves. It is indeed a marvelous act of glorious survival.

1 Corinthians 3:16

HOW HE SEES YOU (PART ONE)

Everything you have experienced and felt that is mind-blowing, astonishing, kind, true, warm, safe, real, full of elation and joy—all of it is directly from Him, custom made to your unique heart. He believes in you; He knows everything about you. No dirt anyone has on you will lessen His love of you.

He grieves with you. He never listens to untruth about you. He is your fan, your protector. He is always for you. He's bringing circumstances together for His glory and your good. He makes no mistakes with you. His tenderness and affection are infinitely greater than what you can fathom. He somehow thinks about you every moment. He's never put off by your unbelief, your distance, or your hiding. He enters into all your pain as though it is His. He never stands aloof. He is, right now, drawing you to hear Him. He is not ashamed of or embarrassed of you. This, and so much more, is how He sees you.

Colossians 3:1-4

HOW HE SEES YOU (PART TWO)

He can be lighthearted with you, if you'd like, right in the middle of your darkest failure. It doesn't seem right, but He has made it right. He will not let life, enemies, opponents, slander, sadness, failure or unbelief swallow you up. He knows exactly when and how to bring water to your desert.

He is not far off but ready and present to meet you in songs of worship and even these words. He has seen all the way down your road, and He smiles. He has good things in store for you. He understands the sorrow, confusions, and disappointments no other human can fully enter into. None of what you're going through is ever punishment or because He doesn't love you as much as another. When confusing misfortune comes, He gathers His angels to watch your faith. He cheers you on. His delight in you is as unique as you are. His power toward and in you is endless. His ownership of you is secure and solid. This is how He sees you.

Psalm 34

HOW HE SEES YOU (PART THREE)

Even in the things you wrongly blame Him for, He does not get angry or defensive. He heaps more grace, more love, more tenderness onto you. Every prayer you cry to Him is fully heard, felt and answered in perfect love. No pain enters your life randomly—but only after the counsel of His love.

You are never left to go it alone, even when you try to walk away. He is holding you, carrying you through every fear, doubt, blinding pain, and devastating disappointment. He is preparing a home unique to your desires and tastes. He will take you Home, to a land where there is no more hurt, no more disillusionment, no more past wounds, no more love promised and not given, no more failure, no more sin. This is how He sees you—always has.

Romans 8:31-39

7.12

WHAT YOU WERE DREAMING

When you're young, God allows you to have many dreams—wild expressions of what could be. You want to change the world. It seems reasonable that should happen soon—like maybe before you're thirty.

You soon realize not all those dreams are going to happen due to the limitations life brings to you—or the limitations you bring. Things like having children, limited finances, your own lack of focus or gifting, health challenges, marrying a person who has their own dreams—for example.

Then another limitation may enter onto the scene: your lack of contentment in what *actually* is. So God changes His tack. He knows your discontent will rob you of the dreams He intends to fulfill in you. Much of the art of living appears to be learning to be content in the dreaming available within the gifting, resources, opportunity, health, relationships, and options your life allows. Trusting God in this way not only gives you contentment, but actually enlarges the realm in which you get to dream.

1 Timothy 6:6-11

HIDE AND SEEK

We can all be self-deceived for a time. We can all carry untruths. God gives us His Holy Spirit and others to help bring those deceptions to light. It's partially why we want to allow others, like counselors and friends, to have access into our lives. They can see what we cannot.

But God never designed you for ruthless soul-searching to discover some secret sin keeping you from full intimacy with Him. That's a largely destructive and colossal waste of time. It presumes that God is holding out on you and will only let you uncover your issues through a promise of enough devotion, and perhaps a season in a Siberian monastery.

God does not desire for you to suffer with a sin hidden from your awareness. He knows how to reveal your stuff to you. He asks only that you not run from Him and others and that you trust Him with what gets revealed. You can rest knowing He is not playing hide-and-seek with you. He wants your health and joy even more than you do.

John 15:9

A TRUE FRIEND

"A true friend is someone who knows the song in your heart and can sing it back to you when you have forgotten the words." (Anonymous)

It's because from early on they've cared about your story so much that it became like their own. They've laughed hard with you, gone on adventures, and laid out under the stars until they knew your tastes, desires, and dreams.

Your view of God is so similar because you've spent scores of hours talking about Him. That friend has owned their influence in your life, to be used by God for your good.

It's true because that friend has drawn closer when you've failed. They were the one standing at your door, wet from the rain, making a joke about how you've ruined their coat. You let them in, and over the next few hours they reminded you who you are, who God is in you, and how much you're needed by so many. They sang words from the song in your heart, and you began to believe again.

1 Samuel 18:1-3

WHO DO YOU WANT TO BE?

What kind of person do you want to be? Not everything is already fixed. Not at all. Within the sovereign goodness of God, you can, at any time, surprise the universe. And everyone around you. Even yourself! Even today, you get to dream about who you want to be, within some physical limitations. Now, if you have blue eyes, you can forget about being president of the Order of Brown Eyes organization.

Maybe best, you can grow into just about any character trait you want. Do you want to be known for your integrity? You can—even if you come from a long line of pickpockets or shady politicians. It won't come from willpower or by writing the word "integrity" on your bathroom mirror. It'll have its best chance by trusting that a person of integrity already lives in you—and living out of that reality. If you've put your faith in Jesus Christ, then you've been rewired, from spiritually dead to spiritually alive and awake. Trust that, and go ahead—surprise the universe.

1 Corinthians 1:30-31

WHEN YOU'RE SICK

You're on an airplane to attend the birthday party of your first grandchild. Perhaps the flu is overtaking you. You discover, again, that as much as you ask, God does not answer your prayer in the manner you'd hoped.

So what do you do with that? Is He not good? Does He not love us? Is He not able? If He won't stave off a little flu, then what are we to do with the biggies?

God wants us to pray, hears our prayers, and loves to give us good things. But apparently *He wants to meet us in our need, not fix all our need.*

Yes, you read that correctly.

We can't see behind the screen. We only know the character of the One behind it. At least some of the time, God responds differently than we want. In the meantime, reach into your pocket for a few Airborne chewables, try to sleep on the flight, and remember nothing, not even the flu, can separate you from His love.

2 Corinthians 12:7-10

RUNNING INTO PEOPLE WHO LEFT YOUR COMMUNITY

We can convince ourselves that our current friends will always be around. "Why would anyone leave? I'm here, and I like me." But they can. Leave. You may eventually find yourself in a community far different than expected.

One day you may meet up with a friend who left. And it will be awkward. "Yep," they seem to imply. "We vacation with our new friends. They are much cooler and way more fun than you. We don't know why we didn't leave sooner. And our new church? It's hipper than yours. Have a nice day."

Some friends need to move on. But others leave when staying would have been healthier for them and the community. Often, deciding to stay or leave is a multifaceted process.

Regardless of our decisions to stay or to leave, God values committed relationships. Our opportunity is to continue learning how He commits to us—and why He does. Then we will increasingly learn how to commit to others, like Jesus.

John 13:34; 17:11

A GENTLE PERSON

One of the great measures of grace in another is that they gradually begin to exhibit the fruit of the Spirit, even against the flow of the values of many cultures and governments. Henri Nouwen captures this beautifully:

Once in a while we meet a gentle person. Gentleness is a virtue hard to find in a society that admires toughness and roughness. We are encouraged to get things done and to get them done fast, even when people get hurt in the process. Success, accomplishment, and productivity count. But the cost is high. There is no place for gentleness in such a milieu.

Gentle is the one who "sees" the other and enjoys being together as much as accomplishing something. A gentle person treads lightly, listens carefully, looks tenderly, and touches with reverence. A gentle person knows that true growth requires nurture, not force. Gentleness dwells within you. You get to choose to express it. In our tough and often unbending world our gentleness can be a vivid reminder of the presence of God among us.

James 3:17

FAMILY OF ORIGIN

We're all inextricably bound together with our families of origin. What they did affects us. The words, actions, and attitudes of your grandparents, parents, aunts, uncles, and siblings have had a formative effect on your life, whether you've completely realized it or not. You'll even find yourself with particular vulnerabilities to certain sins because of them.

But now you have brought Jesus into the equation. Because of your trust in Christ's payment at the cross, you no longer carry a shame identity. You are no longer obligated to play out the downside of your family tree. You're beginning to allow others to help you do the hard work of breaking generational sin and abnormality when irrationality pops up. You're allowing others to more accurately describe reality to you in the midst of chaos. You're believing the power of God to redeem you in the moment. You'll get to see benefit, and your kids may see immense benefit. Over time, the damage from your family line can be broken.

Exodus 34:6-7

THE GREATEST EXPRESSION OF OBEDIENCE

Grace is the only means to enjoy heartfelt, life-freeing obedience to the expressed will of God.

Let's say you get the obedience part. Maybe your problem is that you find yourself judging those who don't. So, fellow traveler, grace for you is to understand that you get to love such folk well and trust God with the timing of their maturity. We can't be certain in any given instance that our application of obedience is fully accurate. That's why the greatest expression of obedience is love. It takes time and often some heartache for any of us to catch on that self-created freedom doesn't satisfy. Loving and not judging give us access into another's life, where God is drawing them to Him. It takes the steam out of a rebellion caused from feeling they are not enough and don't belong.

So, who in your life right now needs you to draw near in love, for the permission to stand with them as God develops obedience in them?

1 John 5:2-3

LISTENING

Listening is a choice of humility—not just for information, but to submit yourself to another's way of seeing. Ever found yourself at a party, in the middle of an intense discussion? Others are sitting nearby, listening. Your ego and pride stand over your shoulder, whispering into your ear. You're reloading while the other person is giving their next statement. Then suddenly you think, *Hey, wait. What she said, that's right! It completely invalidates my position and the structure it was built upon.*

Now you have a choice. You can barge forward, but you'll resort to bluffing and being loud. Or you can admit she's right and ask her to teach you. This is humility in action. Humility promotes respect from others. Humility engenders trust, which engenders transformation. Remember: truth trusted transforms.

Let those of us with ears listen. A beautiful, wise soul said something similar many years ago.

James 1:19-20

SONS AND DAUGHTERS OF GOD

"He predestined us to adoption as sons through Jesus Christ to Himself, according to the kind intention of His will" (Ephesians 1:5).

He's given us previously abandoned ones a family, a place, a home in this galaxy.

We are daughters and sons. Here Paul identifies us as sons, only to explain the rights that belonged exclusively, in Roman society, to an adult son. Now all of us who've believed in Jesus have rights like Roman adult sons. Women, men, girls, boys are now given full heir status, with all past debts cancelled. Suddenly we're given a new name, new resources, a new family history, new status, a legacy, and a future!

Obligation to our past ceases. Our past doesn't cease, but, if we believe this, our past's ability to define us does. Even present failures can't define us. No account of my failures exists anywhere in the public record. Like a thief who washed up onto another planet, you get to be an entirely new you. And every day, you keep washing up again, with no record. How can it be?

Ephesians 1:5

PARENTING WITH-OUT INFLAMING (PART ONE)

God's primary goal is earning our trust so He can love us, increasingly mature us, correct our behavior, and free our lives. We can attempt to offer the same for our children and even teammates. Grace teaches us how to take rebellion out of the equation and replace it with the power of love. How do we address the issue of sin without fanning the flames of religious ought? While each family is unique, here are some ideas to enact such grace-anchored parenting.

Don't ignore behaviors in the name of grace, but face them without condemnation. Weed out the language of the Law: "Why can't you?" "Why won't you?" "What's wrong with you?" Replace yelling with clear, agreed-upon expectations with corresponding consequences. When given, administer discipline with love, commitment, and explanation before and after the event.

Discipline takes the time to explain its reasons and purposes. Never punish to make yourself feel justified. If earning trust is the goal, then grace parenting takes much more time, effort, and intention than winning because we are the parents.

Ephesians 6:4

PARENTING WITH-OUT INFLAMING (PART TWO)

If grace gives us a way to take rebellion out of the equation with our kids and bring love into play, then it's good to imagine some actions that release grace.

Spend lots of time dreaming with them about what the future can look like. Lie in bed together and interact about how life works and why. Explain your relationship with Jesus. Replay the events of the day and try to look through the eyes of others we had conflict with. When the occasion is right, and appropriate to their age, teach them how to depend upon the Spirit's power. Think together about what sacrifice feels like. Admit your own weaknesses and dare to give them permission to speak into your own issues. Talk about owning failure and how you've done it. Consistently tell them how Jesus sees them.

We could convince them that they are as important to us as anything else—and prove it with time and attention. That might be as import-ant as anything else we could do.

1 Thessalonians 1:1-6

PARENTING WITH-OUT INFLAMING (PART THREE)

We can teach our children that Jesus will not humiliate them but guard their hearts. In the moment of conflict, even when they've done wrong, we can get them out of the flammable situation so they can avoid embarrassment and have a chance to respond better.

In that occasion, we get to talk to them about what happens when they become embarrassed or ashamed. We can talk about our own temptations and let them ask questions. We get to grieve with them.

Grace also looks like driving together in the car and challenging gossip, flippancy, values, cynicism, or tattling by reminding them it's not who they are. We can describe how, when they tell on themselves, the consequences will always be different from getting caught.

We get to earn the right to influence by their trust of our integrity. When they fail, we draw even closer, affirm them, bless them. They are in our homes for only a short season. There are few finer gifts than intentionally teaching them a life of grace.

Psalm 23

WHAT IF?

We hide from each other because we're afraid what others would do if they found out the truth about us. It's as old as the Garden. Once Adam sinned, he was afraid of what God would do. Genesis 3:10 says, "I was afraid because I was naked, so I hid myself." So kids learn to hide from their parents, wives from their husbands, employees from their bosses.

But here's the thing: Hiding is like a petri dish for sin. It's where sin grows fastest. But what if it didn't have to be that way? What if parents were able to convince their children that they wanted them to never have to hide? What if, when they tell the truth about what they did, they receive a lesser consequence? What if my child started hiding less, and that corresponded to sinning less?

This single change in our parenting approach protects the hearts of our children and directs our relationships on the path to great goodness.

2 Corinthians 4:2

A DIFFICULT MARRIAGE (PART ONE)

Maybe you woke up this morning unable to pretend any longer. You're in a difficult marriage. You're not sure how much of it is you, how much is your spouse. A hard marriage muddles everything. It's hard to be objective about who's right and who's wrong. All you know is that you wish you weren't married.

Jesus might say to you today, "I saw this day before your wedding, before time. Neither of you are evil, or even intentionally manipulative. You love each other. You just didn't come into the marriage very healthy and you also haven't yet learned how to be married. You don't trust each other's motives, so every action and intention you don't understand is judged. You can still have a wonderful marriage, but you're going to have to open it to Me. You'll also need to let some others in, perhaps including a counselor. But today things can begin to change. You're sick of pretending. If you let Me and others in, your marriage can heal."

Ephesians 5:21

A DIFFICULT MARRIAGE (PART TWO)

You've admitted you're in a difficult marriage. That's step one. You represent millions of marriages. But today is a very good day. You're about to allow God and others in to protect you. What can you expect?

You'll learn how much you need each other. You'll learn love is the process of meeting each other's needs. You'll each discover that you have needs that you cannot meet by yourself. This will rock your world. "Why have I never heard this before? How have I missed this for so long? How would I ever learn to let another meet my needs?"

You'll discover you must trust your spouse to receive their love and they must trust you to receive yours. Close friends will help you start the courageous conversations of how to earn each other's trust. This will be hard. You will often revert to self-sufficient patterns. But you have the power of Christ in you and the protection of trusted friends.

Today won't be easy. But it is a very good day.

Romans 12:9-13

ALIGNMENT

When your steering wheel is crooked while driving straight, your car is likely out of alignment. You may learn to compensate for your wonky drive, and do nothing about it. Life is too full of clamoring matters. But, when your tires start rapidly wearing out on one side, you'll probably give it attention. Now, you've cost yourself some real money.

Throughout life God will give you gentle signs that yours is sliding out of alignment in a given area. These can range from sleeping, rising, eating, working, resting, engaging and retreating from friends, engaging with God and sharing Him, earning money and saving or giving it. All kinds of areas. Like many, you may think, "I'll get to this later." Indeed, "later" comes, but usually with much higher costs.

The beautiful joy of living out of your new identity is you can relax. No need for shame-driven defensiveness. Early-on, you can actually accept that this or that area of your life is out of whack. You can enjoy lower-cost, freeing corrections all through your life.

Mark 6:31-33

LIFE-GIVING COMMUNITIES

Over your lifetime you'll probably have the opportunity to join a number of faith communities. If you pay close attention, there will be a tangible sense to each of them. In some you can feel the over-structured control of the leaders as they seek to create an environment where the members appear well-behaved, together, on their games. Entering, you can feel unsettled, as though nearly everyone there probably fails less than you. That could be your cue to leave.

The objective is *not* to build communities that appear to have sin under control. The objective is to nurture a place where people can stop pretending that they have sin under control.

Entering such a place may feel messy. But it will often also feel welcoming and life-giving. You might experience friends living unedited lives. You might witness perfect love working itself out imperfectly. You might even, over time, be entrusted with stories of maturity and growth that border on the miraculous.

So, as you join, choose wisely. Go toward the life.

Ephesians 4:1-3

"I can have very little meaningful impact upon my family until they begin to trust my influence."

-The Cure & Parents

AUGUST

THIS IS GOD'S OPERATION

Thirteenth-century philosopher Niccolo Machiavelli said, "There is nothing more difficult to take in hand, more perilous to conduct, or more uncertain in its success, than to take the lead in the introduction of a new order of things. Because the innovator has for enemies all those who have done well under the old conditions, and lukewarm defenders in those who may do well under the new. This coolness arises partly from the fear of opponents, who have the laws on their side and partly from the incredulity of men, who do not readily believe in the new things until they have long experienced them."

As we live out the truths of grace, we must remember this is God's operation. He'll get grace to others the way He got it to us—surprisingly and personally. We don't have to sell, push, or argue anyone into God's way of seeing things.

That is God's concern, not ours.

1 Thessalonians 1:5

WHAT YOU HEAR IN THE MIRROR

Try this. Walk into your bathroom and look in the mirror. Take a minute. Get past the blemishes and the discovery that one of your ears is lower than the other. Just look at you.

Now, what would you say to that person you see?

Some of us would confess, "I don't like what I see. I don't trust that expression. I know too much about me to ever enjoy that person in the mirror."

Such a response reflects how we might think God looks at us. We think He'd echo our thoughts: "I'm not pleased. You've got a lot of work to do. You really need to improve in some areas."

But consider this: What if God was looking at you and said, "I really like what I see. I made you exactly to be here right now. Give yourself some slack. And keep looking, for I am doing wonderful things in you."

Now, brush your teeth while you're here. Oh, and you can smile. You should.

1 John 4:19

GOSSIP

"If you don't have anything good to say, come sit by me." A funny line in movies, but few things harm a living community more than gossip.

It takes an intentional theological and relational conviction for a community to be protected in healthy, honest security and faithfulness.

If we believe we have new identities, we can have hope God is developing others' motives. If we believe we're loved equally by God, we can be freed from competition.

If we know our maturity is partially revealed by how we defend the reputation of others, then we will enjoy speaking goodness. If we want others to speak well of us when we are not around, then we will learn to bless them when we are.

Believing these truths, gossip is snuffed out by loyalty: "I have a heart that most wants to love. I will be your defender. Even if you advance beyond me, your achievement is my gain. God has me covered."

And promoting other's good becomes wildly contagious.

Proverbs 20:19

STRONGER THAN YOUR LAZINESS

Every moment of every day, your God is wooing, drawing, and calling out your new heart. He is not compelling you to try harder, strain more, prove your love more, or even trust harder. Instead, He is drawing you to become daily more and more convinced of His love, your new identity, and His power in you to mature you into who He has already made you—righteous, holy, beloved.

He will not be deterred by your failure, laziness, or lack of interest—not even the seditious thoughts you carry, the ones you're sure if He knew He'd have to punish you. He never plans to get even with you. He may shake His head and think, *Now that right there, that was some strong and odd language.*

He has already made up His mind about you, and He will not fail in silently compelling you to that life He intended for you. I know you think you don't deserve such favor. In good time, He will overcome that also. Good luck stopping Him.

Philippians 1:9

OUR DEAR GOD

Even though You are the One who created these moments in us, they're hard to describe back to You. We feel like we're about to explode with joy! They're different from anything else we've found. And we *have* looked. Oh, have we looked.

If we could just get others to feel a moment of what You surprise us with, then all would run to You. It's like living in a dingy one-room flat with sporadic heating in the dead of winter. One day you hear a knock on the door. You open to see a kind man—like Hemingway, but without the issues. He walks in like he owns the place, into the center of the room, and looks deep into your eyes. "I'm so sorry you've had to live like this. I've taken over the place. You're no longer a tenant but a friend. I'm having radiant-heat installed. And I've heard you would like a view. This is not a remodel but a gradual revealing of an entirely new place. Enjoy."

Galatians 2:20

WILLIAM WILBERFORCE

Often God chooses unlikely people to do remarkable things. In the late 1700s William Wilberforce grew up surrounded by wealth, privilege, education, and self-entitled vanity: "As much pains were taken to make me idle as were ever taken to make me studious." Hilarious, huh?

Enamored with politics, he was eventually elected to Parliament. "I did nothing to any purpose. My own distinction was my darling object."

In 1786, God grabbed hold of his heart. Wilberforce found himself wrestling with his life. On Easter Sunday, he put his hope in Christ.

English traders were then raiding the African coast, capturing nearly 50,000 Africans a year, shipping them across the Atlantic to sell into slavery. Before that Easter Sunday, this had mattered little to Wilberforce.

His education, political acumen, and charisma were then reshaped for meaning. His tireless efforts led to the eventual abolishment of the slave trade in the British Empire.

God wastes nothing in our lives. He's always right on time, reshaping our talents and training for goodness. It's what God does.

Jeremiah 18:4

8.6

BACK IN BUSINESS

When a leader and/or an employee begins to try grace out in their business, it can now have a clear avenue to get modeled, taught and released. Grace soon creates a fragile but genuine environment of safety. At first this feels unusual but also surprisingly welcome. God shows up in the workplace without a company-wide email notification.

Many employees have not experienced a lot of grace. Their world is too often run by a toxic combination of blame and fear. But because of the very affirming and encouraging nature of grace, it is soon embraced by Christians and non-Christians alike.

The use and presence of grace in the workplace is endorsed, protected, and grown by God in ways we can't imagine. Trusting God to protect and deliver on our behalf while we exercise grace is beautiful and rewarding. It doesn't mean everything will always run smoothly. Grace is messy. But it does mean that grace has a chance to be authentic, life-giving, and productive for your particular workplace.

Suddenly God is back in business, so to speak.

Colossians 3:23

DO YOUR THING

Have you noticed that sunglasses make everyone look better? It brings up an interesting question: Is it wrong to want to look fashionable? One of the great things about life in grace is that you don't have to play pretend. It's fine to have no interest in current styles.

It isn't fine to judge those who do.

When it comes to fashion, everyone gets to do their thing. God loves it all. Just don't say, "Well, look at Jesus. He dressed plainly." We don't know that. Isaiah says He came humbly. That doesn't mean He didn't pay attention to His appearance.

Caring how you look can be an indicator of health and freedom. This is knowing you're loved, not vanity. If you're convinced He adores you, then you might not dress as one who feels unloved. Your freedom might also give you permission to stop worrying about your appearance. You need not dress any particular way. You get to be yourself. There's no virtue in any particular fashion or lack of fashion. What grace gives you is style. You're loved. Do your thing.

Ecclesiastes 9:7-9

LOW-GRADE DISGUST

The traits that seem to bother us most in others are often the ones we are most disgusted with in ourselves.

The choice of the word "disgusted" is intentional. If we believe that God continually carries a low-grade disgust of us, then we'll probably carry a similar disgust of ourselves. But that disgust is a lot to carry around. We can't bear to keep seeing ourselves as failures. Surely someone else must be worse than we are. So the search begins. It doesn't take long to find many others to be disgusted with.

There's another way. God sees all the issues in your life, not with a view to condemn, but only to care for you. How can it be that God knows all your stuff and still adores you like He does His only Son? It's impossible to fully wrap our heart around that. But if you can believe it even a little, then self-disgust begins to vanish. Everyone around you will catch a break—be free from judgment. So will you.

Romans 4:7-8

LIMITATIONS

As children we sensed that limitations in us, or anything appearing weak, were to be avoided, denied, or hidden. Limitations in us were proof that we didn't belong or had to be pitied.

But what if our needs and limitations are essential to receiving love?

What if God intentionally created each of us with limitations so we could receive love?

Now, when you're on your game and don't sense need, you are essentially self-sufficient. And while you may be admired, you may not experience much love. For if love is essentially the process of meeting another's needs, then nobody gets to love you unless they are invited in to protect or stand with you in areas of limitation.

Today, think about your limitations and see them as gifts from God for you. Also think about how you can allow someone to love you in your limitations—your friends are patiently waiting for the opportunity.

2 Corinthians 12:7-10

PRICE CHECK ON REGISTER FOUR

Many have experienced this odd, seemingly impossible quirk in the universe. It's happened often enough to no longer be denied. Whichever line you pick in the supermarket turns out to be the longer line. "Price check on register four!" The line you're now trapped in. Several minutes later, you look over to see the people who joined line three, *after* you joined four, are checked out and heading home. It can make you feel like the entire cosmos conspired against you, that karma is a real thing, or that God has had it out for you for something you did in high school.

Seriously, there's no karma. And God's not paying you back for the soda you didn't pay for at prom. Nope. You're simply part of a broken planet. And even when there's a price check on register four, God is working everything for His glory and your best.

Romans 8:31-32

UNSEEN CONSTRUCTION

It's fascinating to watch a home go up in your neighborhood. At first, there's lots of activity, as they scrape the remnants of the existing lot. Big trucks and noise. Then nothing, for weeks. Did the foreman forget the address? Some executive-looking types in ties show up to chat. Days later a group strolls in to look at blueprints. Then a crew digs, lays wire, and marks off perimeters.

Seasons pass. Another crew buries all but a few pipes. Neighbors gossip that maybe these people aren't professionals. One day cement trucks show up and a foundation is poured. Then the wood arrives. Within 48 hours an entire home is framed! Suddenly, it's going to be amazing!

So it is with our maturing. Much is happening you can't see. New wiring was connected to power. One day friends will see framing go up even before you do. You'll all feel a little foolish that you doubted the project. So for now, relax and trust the Owner, Designer, and Foreman. This place is going to have serious curb appeal.

Mark 4:30-32

A SURPRISING WIN

The grace of Jesus is attracted anytime we discover we can't do some-thing we were previously convinced we could. Jesus is able to lean closest whenever the veneer of self-sufficiency leaves us feeling unex-pectedly vulnerable, clumsy, and unable. What a surprising revelation! We might have thought He would have been drawn by our triumphant wins. He does inhabit those also. But need that creates dependency brings Him running into our fears and self-doubts. It's a stunning de-velopment for those of us who haven't had a win in a while.

There is no gain in pretending to Him that you are doing better than you are. Tell Him all of it. He already knows, and you telling Him makes it more real to you. He will not leave you hanging. Although He indwells you fully and always, He comes running the moment you get it out. You could do it today, right now.

1 Peter 5:5-7

DUCKING CONFLICT

God never desires that we ignore the conflict that could lead to resolution. But we get good at avoiding messiness. We've all been hurt too many times. And we've all hurt others too many times. Wading in to carry out the elephant in the room, we discover the elephant got bigger and several Bengal tigers slipped in.

But Christ in us has the last say in this room. He is working for authentic, healed friendships that can affirm, protect, speak into, and defend hearts. Some of the best friendships risked staying in the room even when truth was hard to hear and share, and while things remained unresolved.

They dare to believe Jesus is supernaturally able to undo self-vindication and self-protection. Note to self: This often doesn't happen in the first attempt. Or the fourth.

Healing and freedom can happen if we step into that room with the humility of Christ in us. It will never happen if we always choose to evade the elephants and tigers.

Ephesians 4:1-3

FAILING WELL

The ultimate goal is not to keep another from failing. The goal is to help them fail well.

We will all fail. Often. The objective of friendship is to give the other a safe place to fail well. An environment that anticipates and is ready to draw close will ensure that failure does not become the identity of the one who fails.

When we become convinced we are a failure at our core, we give ourselves permission to fail as a way of life. Why not? We're a failure anyway.

We get to convince each other our failure does not change our actual identity as beloved. We can see ourselves as completely remade creations who still, sometimes, fail.

Then we are freer to create and risk, wildly trying out our gifting and capacity, surrounded by those who anticipate failure. But they also are anticipating incredible goodness and success. Why? Because we are free to try out who we are—and who we are, when not afraid of the consequences of failure, is absolutely stunning!

Galatians 5:15-26

SOMETIMES VERY MUCH BETTER

Wherever you are right now, you're not alone. God Himself enters into each second. You are cherished in this very moment! God is giving His very Person for you to lean into. There are no lectures. He cares more about your battle than you do. Yes, run hard, love intensely. But relax, even in the crunch of it. Let Him love you. Let Him protect you. You've nothing left to atone for.

Express worth to others, even in the midst of your storm. For a moment, let go of how behind you feel. Walk outdoors and breathe deeply. You were made for this time. This confidence is more important than whatever you woke up fearing.

Look, you couldn't even figure out how to find God. He found *you*. Did you think He'd forget how to care for you? It won't always look like what you hoped. But time will show it's sometimes very much better.

1 John 4:16-18

EPIPHANIES

Periodically, you may find yourself watching a movie. Suddenly a scene catches you off guard and causes you to experience a truth you'd previously only experienced in a mental way. But now you enter into the concept. You can see it, feel it, sense it like never before. You are receiving a God perspective that leaves you undone. As you reflect later, it can change your plans for the evening, and sometimes the rest of your life.

Theologians describe this as an *epiphany*—those moments when your new nature cries out, "Wow! God, that was You, wasn't it?" You cannot schedule them or will them into existence. But you can be more intentional about surrounding yourself with life-giving, soul-evoking sources that, through their craft and gifting, inspire and evoke that place where God transcendently invades your experience. This might involve you saying no more often to distractions. It might involve asking what sources help you meet with God.

You cannot plan epiphanies. But you may be able to woo them.

Isaiah 6

ONE OF THE LAST FEARS TO GO

Perhaps one of the last fears about God to be dismantled is that He might retaliate, or pay back, for something wrong you say or think.

Let's say, out of the blue, an odd, violating sexual thought comes to your sudden awareness. The next thought for many is, *Whoa! What's wrong with me? I'm going to so pay for this!* Or you say something flippant about God in casual conversation and then wonder when and how you will be paying for that particular indiscretion, believing He keeps copious track of every misplaced thought or word to someday be used against you.

The cross and resurrection created a relationship with God that vanquishes all such nonsense. He is not peevish, oversensitive, or vindictive. *Nothing* you will ever experience is a knee-jerk, pay-back response from God. He knows your heart. He knows your place of maturity. And He knows His love for you.

This is gospel, the best news. Don't be afraid.

Psalm 103:12-13

8.18

AN AUTHORITY STRONGER THAN YOU

Can the Bible be trusted? So much has been written about the inspiration of the scriptures. For a moment, give yourself permission to ditch the arguments. Here's the rub: Either you have a completely trustworthy authority stronger than you, or you're still your own authority. There's not an in-between.

While no one can tell you what it'll take to put your weight on His Word, pretending to believe what you do not helps no one. Cognitive dissonance cannot long be endured.

Many of us encounter fear, shame, moralism, and self-condemnation when we read the Bible. Man imposed that—not God. God wants you to be lifted up and led through His Word. While there are many things we will never perfectly understand, the story of God's pursuit and redemption of His world and His people is more than inspiring. It is the inspired work of our Creator.

Hebrews 4:12-13

YOU WERE NOT INVITED

Apparently there was a big party recently in your community. Many of your friends were there. You wouldn't have known about it except several asked why you couldn't make it. You weren't invited. This is not the first, or second, time you've not been invited. So, what do you do with that? You can pretend you don't care, but you do. You can pretend you understand their rationale, but you don't. Why would they exclude you?

This is one you'd best not try to solve on your own. This is where trusted friends get to speak to you for God. You may discover the reasons have little to do with you. Or it might be that you're at odds with a friend common to the community. Or you might hear, "Sometimes, some people don't always feel safe around you." Ouch. Then you get to give that friend permission into your life maybe more than ever before.

The gift of being kindly told what you otherwise cannot see? Priceless. You are being loved well by God, through a friend.

Luke 14:12-15

VULNERABILITY

There's always been the misconception that mature Christians are in control, not needy, and on their game. There is some truth to this. Christ in us eventually brings order from chaos. But our Champion made Himself vulnerable for our sakes. He was not vulnerable in whiny self-centeredness. Instead, He chose to trust His Father for His strength. It left Him without self-protection in a mean and mocking world.

Dependent trust is the way of our Savior. He could've avoided so much pain and looked like the dominating God we assumed He'd be. Instead, He allowed Himself to be dependent so we could learn strength in our God.

When we choose to live unashamed of what's revealed, we're declaring that God's timing, pace, and sufficiency are fully enough. We're not to know each other in independent sufficiency, no matter how good it looks. We are to love each other in our susceptibilities. Not every person needs to know these. But some need to know you without pretense. This is largely how the world knows we belong to Him.

Luke 22:42-43

THE HOWL

There's a howling voice built into the world's system. It's attempting to convince you there's a universal, pulsing drumbeat of the successful. The voice hisses that if you don't pull it together, you're going to fall hopelessly behind. You will be a failure.

This is not the voice of Proverbs reminding us to avoid laziness while being diligent toward work and healthy achievement. This howl will not be satisfied by any amount of accomplishment. The more you run after it, the further behind you will feel. It will leave you exhausted, discouraged, and guilty, and not quite sure why.

God's design values diligence and healthy work. He's wired you for accomplishing good. But working faithfully actually invigorates you! There is no crack of a whip. There's time to accomplish His will, peace, and joy, plus the time it takes to develop meaningful relationships of grace.

You, friend, each day, get to decide which voice to follow.

1 John 2:15-17

GIVING YOU HONOR

Hi. It's Me again.

I inspired Paul to write a very strong statement in Romans 8. It is about how I, God, cause all things to ultimately work out better than if they'd never happened. I know that sounds impossible. Especially when you're in the middle of ongoing pain or grief.

You might feel there must be something wrong with you. Most everyone else seems pretty on their game. It doesn't make any sense. So you ask, "What's wrong with me?"

On that day on a hill centuries ago, I overcame the shame that wants to define you.

This pain you are experiencing? It is never proof of something wrong with you.

And it is also never about the failure of My love for you. My love for you is personal and unchangeable.

None of this takes away the pain you're feeling. I know this. But I wanted you to know I'm always forging beauty through it. So maybe, even today, you might face it with bravery and honor.

Love,
God

1 Peter 1:6-9

A BEAUTIFUL THING

You've started to trust this way of life in grace. You no longer have to prove yourself to God by enough prayer or Bible reading. At first, it's so freeing. But maybe you've noticed recently that it's been a week or so since you read your Bible. And you're not praying as much as you did. It's easy to think, *Hey, wait! My motive may have been screwy but at least I was reading my Bible.* You did have a way to convince yourself you were good with God. So, you may want to return to that way of living.

Before you do, consider that your new heart responds to thirst. Maybe it's never had a chance to get thirsty. This is common when we continually keep ourselves under self-imposed regulations. God's method of drawing us is through longing. Longing causes activity. We find ourselves reading the Bible and talking to God now because it fulfills our longing, not because we're trying to prove anything. We got thirsty enough.

Thirst. It's a beautiful thing.

Psalm 63:1

NEW EYES

One day soon we will be in heaven. Imagine that! And we'll have new eyes. We'll see everything better and more clearly. Categorically different.

Maybe there won't be new colors. Maybe God already gave us all the colors. Imagine that! But on that day we'll see color the way we were hoping colors could look—the way God originally intended.

Kind of like how we're hoping to one day see each other.

"Hey, wait! You're Jenny Swanson, aren't you?" "Why, yes, I am."
"I knew it! You were an absolute mess on Earth. But all of us who loved you, we could see it in you."
"See what?"
"I guess, what you would be like in heaven. Even at your worst we could see it."
"Wow!"
"You know what?" "What?"
"We were right."

Imagine that.

Colossians 3:4

WHY PLANT TREES

There is a man named Garth who moved to West Africa years ago for a job with a radio ministry. When he arrived, the ministry bought a large section of poorly managed land, and Garth started doing something bizarre—he began planting trees.

Methodically, carefully, he planted thousands each year in this area. A few years later difficult times came, and it seemed likely that he would lose his radio job. His future in the country became questionable. Still, he humbly kept planting.

An amazing thing began to happen in this re-birthed forest. Hundreds of species began returning to the refuge of his trees. People from nearby areas began to tend and care for the growing forest alongside Garth. A healthy, thriving ecosystem started to emerge.

Many people would have stopped planting trees when the future looked rocky. They might even have packed up. But Garth continued to invest in the future of others, even if it might not be his future. So keep planting—others will need your trees.

Philippians 2:4

RECALIBRATING WITH CHILDREN

"Having children has been by far the kindest and most unifying time in our marriage," said no one ever. As delightful and rewarding as children are, they bring stratospheric relational chaos and insufficient sleep to even the healthiest of marriages. You discover that the person you dearly loved and chose to marry can now make you fully exasperated. You seem to resent them the most when your child is awake in the middle of the night or throwing spaghetti around the living room. Usually the one with the most sleep makes this correlation.

You still love each other very much. Parenting is simply exposing that you do not agree with each other on everything. Faux expressions of love are not helpful, but you could break the spell with a tangible act of love—maybe a verbal peace offering, such as, "I'd still marry you all over again. This is hard, but I'd rather go through this with you than with anyone else."

Psalm 127:3-5

CONVERSATIONS JESUS MIGHT HAVE HAD

(With His disciples along the road from Joppa to Jericho)

Bartholomew: "May I be honest?"

Jesus: "Of course."

Bartholomew: "I don't like unleavened bread much. It's dry. And it breaks to pieces in a satchel."

Jesus: "My friend, I can't fully explain this to you yet, but soon the Gentiles are going to come into the picture. And when they do, they will bring yeast with them."

Bartholomew: "I'm not sure I—"

Jesus: "I have one word for you. It won't help you, but it's gonna be a game-changer for your great-great-great-great-great-grandchildren."

Bartholomew: "What's the word?"

Jesus: "Doughnuts."

Bartholomew: "Doughnuts?"

Jesus: "That's all I can say for now: doughnuts. And I'd appreciate it if you didn't share this with the others."

Bartholomew: "Sure. Doughnuts, huh?"

Jesus: "Verily. Doughnuts."

This is the last time the matter was spoken of. But every now and then Bartholomew and Jesus nodded knowingly to each other.

Deuteronomy 29:29

8.28

MERCY ME

"Christianity is the only religion, whose God bears the scars of evil." This historic insight from Os Guinness holds true largely because our God is rich in mercy. God's mercy compels Him to relieve the suffering of the hurting, the marginalized, and even the evil offender—no matter what it costs Him.

Mercy is God's natural instinct. Now, it's your core instinct too. You may have lived a hard, indifferent life toward others, but Jesus gave you a new identity. He has the scars to prove it. Now, the new you longs to show mercy.

Your flesh wants nothing to do with your new-mercy heart, because showing mercy is messy and costly. So, it may take awhile to live into this, but you will show exquisite mercy many times in your life. You have new eyes to see the suffering.

By the way, it takes wisdom to offer lavish mercy, so invite the Spirit to guide your mercy actions. Often, He will use your trusted friends to suggest when and how to show God's extravagant mercy.

1 Peter 1:3

LIVING WITH CHRIST AND ADDICTION

How can these two realities even coexist in me?

We who have Christ in us *all* suffer from addiction. Apart from medical reasons, the same dynamics that propel substance addiction also drive compulsive habits or repeating sins—such as addiction to possessions, moods, power, sex, anger, bitterness, clinging, withdrawal, grasping, stubbornness, being right, reputation, gambling, un-repentance, un-forgiveness, gossip, lying, jealousy, denial, revenge, cheating, attractiveness, manipulation, fantasies, and much more.

We'll do anything to replace God and our intimacy with Him Simply understanding addiction will not free us, but it will point us to our only hope: grace—drawing us back to the Source, Jesus. The Source is stronger than our shame-driven addictions.

By the kindness of His grace, God is teaching us that our addiction, rather than being a barrier, is actually a bridge to bring us into the beauty, intimacy, and pleasure with Him that we have always deeply longed for. While addiction is complex, God's kindness reveals our "homesickness" and compels us to return from our wanderings.

Romans 2:4

COURAGE

It took courage to go to sleep without the hall light on. It took courage when your parents moved to a new town and you had to insert yourself into another circle of friends. It took courage to ask anyone to a school dance. It takes courage to try something you could fail miserably at.

Courage. It's doing something that frightens you. It's standing in the face of pain or grief. All humans are capable of it, but there appears to be a courage required for believers that exceeds natural bravery. "In the world you will have tribulation, but take courage; I have overcome the world." The world's system, in its opposition to God, creates a need for a particular courage in believers.

It takes courage to face mocking of your faith. It takes courage to face eternity, no matter how much we've been taught heaven is real. Jesus created a basis for your courage by overcoming the worst life can present—death itself. Take courage, friends.

John 16:33

SEPTEMBER

"What if there was a place so safe that the worst of me could be known, and I would discover that I would not be loved less but more in the telling of it?"
-The Cure

IF ONLY

Many of us feel stuck, living in the aftermath of an immature or missed choice. If only we had married that person, or not taken that job, or, well, you name it. If only . . .

Our choices cannot always be measured by the consequences following them. Or the most significant choice of Christ's life would have initially appeared to be a failure.

Yes, intentional choices of sin bring consequences. But even those become highlights of God's restorative love.

From the moment you choose, it becomes the choice God is working in. That choice is now what is. "If only" thinking is a colossal waste. Musing over a better life God might have had for you robs you of fully engaging in the life that is. This is your best life, right now. When it's not, He will direct you from it, change the situation, or teach you to live transcendently in what is.

Choose wisely. And the wisest choice is trusting that God is powerful, good, and committed to your freedom.

Jeremiah 32:17

GRACE IS MESSY

Legalism and religious moralism look all neat and clean because most of the failure is hidden. Grace has a way of taking failure out of the darkness and into the light.

So here you are, risking this life of grace. You used to present pretty slick, back in the days of religious performance. Inside, you knew better. But you appeared pretty put-together.

Then you started seeing differently. You discovered God wanted you to live authentically more than appear perfect. Now you can't go back. You've experienced too much that is real. It's hard for so much of your messed-up stuff to be out there for everyone to see. But even this can't deter you.

God already knew about all your messed-up stuff. He delights in watching you risk this life of grace, loving and being loved. He knows that health and goodness and authenticity are being formed in you.

Sure, it's messy, but it's not slick. You're better than slick.

1 John 1:5-10

IDOLS

You may be tempted to identify your idols and then, one by one, with watchful diligence and slavish intention, eradicate, be freed, or released from them.

Jesus might kindly say to you, "In truth, you just created another idol—your confidence in your ability to vanquish your idols. Your idols will not be eradicated by good intention and rigorous self-examination but by substitution. You created them because you could not yet believe that I am who I say I am in you. When you see me well, when you see the beauty of my delight, the freedom of this life in the light, the idols will begin to lose their shape, form and pull. There are many who want you to focus on naming and destroying your idols. I wish you wouldn't bother. These idols exist only because you are still too frightened to risk substituting the old life with the one I want us to enjoy together. I'll never stop inviting you to join Me."

1 John 5:21

WHEN OUR CHILD EMBARRASSES US

Maybe it's your daughter, at your local public library, when she loudly tries out a word she heard this week at school.

Maybe it's your son, at your new neighbor's dinner table, saying, "Whatever this is, I'm not eating it. It smells like pee."

We get embarrassed by our children. Triggered.

Sometimes we blow up at them. Yell at them. We're bigger, right?

But our over-reaction is not about them. And they know it. We do too.

Nothing can trigger shame like our kids. They are supposed to be the proof that we do parenting well. How dare they show the public we're not as together as we try to present!

Here's graceful parenting: Own it. Tell your child the over-reaction was about you. Your children are wired to trust you. And confession like that takes shame out at the knees.

God says something like, "I can handle exactly where your family is right now. I am not embarrassed by any of you. I stand with My arm around all of you."

Ephesians 6:4

WHEN OUR PARENTS EMBARRASS US

If your parents haven't yet, just wait. They will embarrass you.

At some point most parents lose the narrative. It's not just that they're no longer cool. It's more that they become less self-aware. They can't as easily hear themselves as they moralistically teach you at each turn.

They can become the brunt of family humor—because they are parents and are supposed to be strong enough to take it.

But they're not. They get hurt, though they might not say it. They fear losing their seat at the table.

You are the one who can protect them.

Love proclaims that you're still needed. It's what every aging parent clamors after.

Love says you'll always have a place, that you are worthy of not being ridiculed or ignored, even when you're less relevant.

Then an interesting phenomenon can happen: The parent doesn't try so hard. They stop embarrassing you as often.

Or maybe they're the same as always. Maybe it's you who has changed.

1 Corinthians 13

WHEN YOU EMBARRASS YOURSELF

Shame can be partially explained as the next thing that happens once you get embarrassed. It can make us feel stupid and utterly unloveable.

It sounds like religious hocus-pocus to read that Jesus took your shame upon Him and defeated it, giving you a brand-new, shame-free identity.

What about Jesus dying on a cross could take away what happens when I get embarrassed?

Before Jesus became your sin, when the real you got embarrassed, the nakedness you felt was accurate. You were a person rightly accused and accurately defined in shame.

But from the moment Jesus took up residence inside, you are no longer that person. You are "Jesus in you." The shame was paid for. You now carry His righteousness. So you can't be accused of being a person who rightly carries shame. And you can no longer be defined as a loser defined by shame.

You may still feel it. It's just no longer accurate. Once you start to believe your righteousness, you don't get embarrassed as easily.

For you know who you are.

Hebrews 12:2

9.6

A CASE FOR OUTLANDISH LAUGHTER

We've all heard the hollow, loud, brutish laughter of people we'd rather not be around. Huge, unbridled laughter can come from the likes of womanizers, gossipers, and telemarketers. We are exhorted, as the people of God, to not be like them. So we rein in our big laughter.

But laughter is not the culprit here. Laughter pouring from God's people powerfully expresses this new life within us. One of the great permissions of free people is to laugh and laugh, sometimes until tears fill our eyes and we can't catch our breath.

Those who guard, hide, or perform for enough acceptance from God and man understandably have less to laugh about. They are miserable in their religion. It makes people wonder why anyone would choose a religion that makes them look like they have a headache all the time.

Even in a tragic world, we are freed people with much to laugh about. It reveals our health and hope. We have permission to laugh loudly, like happy drunks—but without the hangover.

1 Peter 1:8-9

9.7

GIVING DIGNITY

One of the great evidences of grace sacredly alive is how we express dignity. We're asked to represent God by giving dignity to all simply because they're made in the image of God. It's easy to honor the famous and highly accomplished. To give honor to those in common or subservient roles displays a love not owned by a performance-driven doctrine. Love chooses its friends and those to admire based on something stronger than social strata or financial net worth.

You can look into the eyes of one who has served you well at a checkout counter and say, "Thank you for thoughtfully serving me." Or you can periodically hand several extra dollars to the person operating your carwash, saying, "I've seen you here a lot. You always smile at me and do such good work. Thank you." It's only a few dollars, but it tells them that you value something deeper than position.

James 2:2-13

CHERISH IS THE WORD

One of humanity's most enjoyable statements is penned by the apostle John. But then you realize just how perfect and supremely healthy it is. In John 13:23 he says, "There was reclining on Jesus' bosom one of His disciples, whom Jesus loved."

It's so heartwarming. In essence he's saying, "You know who I'm talking about, right? Me, *John.* The one whom Jesus loved." How spectacular! John actually thought Jesus' unique love for him was his distinguishing identification. What's amazing is that every disciple would have said the same about himself. Almost every person who ever met Jesus no doubt felt that way!

John was describing what it feels like to be cherished, not certain if anyone else is loved by Him as much!

This is the reception of love—to see yourself as the beneficiary of God's boundless affection. John knew he hadn't earned it. He just knew that even if no one else in the world was loved completely, he was.

We get to say the same of ourselves—*cherished*. Go ahead. Try it.

John 13:23

9.9

NO NEED TO PANIC

Lets say you just woke up one day and realized, "I haven't really been thinking about God much at all lately." Okay, now what happens next is really important. Shame will without a hint of hesitation rush in and whisper, "See, this proves it. There is definitely something wrong with you. C'mon, who would ignore the One who loves them so much?"

Here's a grace-filled response to practice: "Well, apparently people who love God drift at times. Knowing Jesus was willing to go to the cross for only me, I know He adores me continually. I imagine He'd really love to hear from me right now. I'm going to believe He's not mad or disgusted or that there's some punishment waiting in the wings. I still don't feel much like reading His Word right now, but I'm going to gamble that He can handle that. He just wants the real me. That's all He's asking for. I can give Him that."

God is really hoping you will respond to yourself with grace.

John 15:9,15

WHEN EVENING COMES

Few moments are more transcendent than finding yourself still and alone with God when evening comes. You can't predict the experience. Your permission is to show up.

David knew this experience. Often. "May my prayer be counted as incense to You! The lifting up of my hands as the evening offering." He's asking God to receive his prayer in all the beauty, sincerity, and love in which he knew it was being offered. He already knows the answer to his request. He's just letting God hear what they both know is happening. He's experiencing the God who is always there.

This same God shows up every evening. You get to set the stage and create the location. You invite God into the moment He has already prepared for you. The end of the day is a marvelous time to say, "My God, thank You for the gift of this day, and that includes right now. I trust You with everything and with me. I hope You're enjoying sitting here together as much as I am."

Psalm 141:1-2

A TALE OF TWO GENERATIONS

The older generations were taught something so they could tell something. The gospel became a message.

The younger generations want to receive something so they can become something. Many are not certain the older generations have much to give them.

And the older generations know it. They've grown older but not always wiser.

But what matters is that all generations can still vitally find each other. The pathway is humility.

In humility, the older generations could ask permission to learn from the younger generations. Their younger friends carry much-needed perspectives and wisdom.

In humility, those from the younger generations could risk letting their elders find a way back home. The older generations have much to offer. Jesus has been working vitally in them for the moment of such awakenings.

It may be easier to reinvent community over and over every several decades. How much healthier and more accessible we'd be to the world if they could see us, older and younger, loving and learning from each other.

1 John 2:12-14

ALL YOUR NEEDS

"And my God will supply all your needs" (Philippians 4:19).

If that's true, and it most certainly is, the following most certainly are also:

- If you don't have it, you don't yet need it.
- If He doesn't give it, there might be a very good reason you don't want it.
- If you don't have it but do need it, you'll probably be getting it soon.
- If you have it and don't want it, then it is probably doing something very wonderful in you.
- If you have it and Jesus can't use it for something very helpful, then He'll probably free you from it very soon.
- If you have it and it's bad, He can turn it into something used for good.
- If you caused it and it's bad, then He can turn that into something used for good.

Romans 8

THE LONELY PEOPLE

This is for all the lonely people.

Alone because of setback or loss. Alone because of chemical prisons. Alone because of _____ (fill in the blank).

Here's hope. Our God in Jesus became lonelier and more alone than any of us ever will.

What He accomplished allows Him to completely experience and enter into your exact loneliness.

You will never out-lonely Him.

More important, He makes the astonishing promise to be fully there, in your deepest loneliness. You may argue that it doesn't matter if you can't have tangible presence.

But are you certain?

Imagine that you're alone in a strange land; nobody knows you. If you were convinced your best friend was cupping hands around your face, whispering how much she loves and cherishes you, even though you could not see her, then wouldn't you feel marvelously less alone?

Chances are good you would.

This is your reality in the middle of your particular aloneness—if only you could be convinced.

Today's a good day to get alone and ask God if this could possibly be true.

Mark 15:34

TWENTY-THREE MILLION LATTES

Many of us have days when we wonder, *Did it take? I know I say I know Jesus, but am I sure? My behaviors and attitudes much of the time don't display it.*

Consider this: Say that someone could legitimately get you twenty-three million lattes. Also, no pain for the rest of your life. And free. Plus you get to go to heaven. There's only one condition: For the rest of your life you may not talk to or listen to God. You can't read His Word or maintain any thoughts about Him or His love. So, what do you say?

Most of us would at least entertain the notion. Some of us might take the offer. But probably, eventually, those of us who've put our faith in Jesus, as much as we might want the free lattes, would have to say no.

Crazy, huh? We'd even turn down a pain-free existence to continue a dialogue with the God we cannot see and often cannot feel. Well then. Perhaps this relationship with God really did take.

1 Peter 1:17-21

9.15

EARNING BACK TRUST (PART ONE)

So what happens now? You've forgiven him, for your benefit. He's owned the damage and hurt he caused before God for his benefit and to be right with you. Healing is happening.

But something's still not right. Trust is still lagging behind.

It should. It'll be raw for a while. Forgiving is not the same as trusting. There's no magic wand to make trust reappear. Trust is rebuilt without a timeline. You can only want to allow it. You can't coerce it.

Trust must be rebuilt better than the last time. The conversation could begin like this: "I believe your apology. I really do. And it's hard to admit this, but I still need you. I want us back, closer than ever. I'm not counting on 100 percent perfection. I'm counting on you trusting God with your failures. I'm asking for the same in me. This will take bravery. To fully tell the truth. I want to rebuild trust—at least, most of the time."

Hebrews 13:18-19

EARNING BACK TRUST (PART TWO)

Yesterday, we tried to express what opening the door to trust might look like from the side of the one who was hurt. But what about the one who caused the pain, repented of their guilt, and was restored? How does he or she begin to find the way to restored trust?

It might go like this: "I know what I've done to you. I still detest it. I can't undo it. But I'm allowing God to restore me. I'm trusting Him to reveal new implications of how I hurt you. What got missed in the pain is that I still need you, a lot. I'm going to be weird at times. I easily run back to my shame. But if you'll believe the sincerity of my heart, I think God will allow me to get it right more often. Will you stand with me in this? I'm all in."

Ephesians 4:30-32

EARNING BACK TRUST (PART THREE)

You were hurt. Your trust was broken. It was real. The journey back to trusting can be treacherous. There is a subtle posture you can fall into—that of the victimized innocent one. This unspoken position can be an enemy to restoration.

"Yes, I've forgiven her. But it'll never be the same. The damage has been done. I will try to be here for her but from a distance. At the end of the day, she's still the same person. I don't think I'll ever fully trust her again."

We can have this conversation with God and think He's okay with it. We can justify it. But here's a gentle challenge: Have that conversation with a trusted friend who loves both you and the one who hurt you. They can help you reevaluate your logic and motives. If you let them, they'll guide your good heart to where it most wants to go. They'll protect you. This is facing pain without faking it, and you're going to need trusted others close by.

Galatians 6:1-2

SAFE NOT SOFT

Grace is where the truth can flow most freely. When God invites you into His throne room of grace, He's welcoming you into a safe environment. Here you can share the truth about how you are doing, so mercy and grace can help you in your time of need. This includes working on the truth about your stuff, which can be arduous and full of hope.

So, grace is a safe place, *not* a soft place. Grace is for your healing and growth. This is another reason why grace suits the marketplace. Even in job reviews, a loving supervisor who's committed to your best can assume the same position God has with you, standing with you to affirm you, even as they continue to develop you in an area of weakness. As Hud McWilliams declares in his exceptional book, "Grace provides a vehicle for that to occur." This joyful truth holds enormous implications. Everyone in the next business, refugee camp or ministry you walk into needs this too-rare message of safe, not soft.

Ephesians 4:1-16

GARMAN'S PUB (PART ONE)

Veer off the exceptionally bland I-5 freeway north of L.A. and onto California 126 toward Ventura, and you'll suddenly be driving by fruit stands every mile or so. In about thirty miles, you'll come upon Santa Paula, a delightful throwback town with a grand mix of ethnicity and history. Halfway down its main street sits Garman's Pub. In some ways it's like other good pubs: dart boards, cable sports, exceptional beer, a world-class variety of whiskeys, and killer burgers. An art-deco mirror runs parallel along the length of the masterfully restored bar counter.

In the evenings, standing behind that counter, is the owner, Clint Garman. He and his wife, Gina, make this particular pub different from most. Clint's a man of mature and practical faith. Growing up, he envisioned a place where anyone could access God's grace and love in a setting most might not expect. Weddings, funerals, dedications, and Bible studies take place in his pub. The venture is not without risks and objections. But the attempt to merge faith and community God must surely find delightful.

1 Peter 2:12

9.20

GARMAN'S PUB (PART TWO)

Most often the sacred and the secular tend to stay in their own lanes. God longs for them to merge. How else would Jesus be seen, except by non-believers forced to find their way onto the turf of believers?

Clint Garman and a community of like-hearted friends are trying for the merge. Faith shows up on the home field of those who might never otherwise see church. Often there's no blueprint and more disagreement than answers. Clint embraces the tension. He reasons that it's better for him, who embodies Jesus, to be at the counter when a loud white-supremacist angers a group of locals. He recalls such an evening: "I leaned over the bar and whispered, 'So, it doesn't look good for you at this moment. Would you like me to help?'" The man nodded. Clint spoke words of wisdom and peace to the entire room, all with the kind smile of a man everyone trusts and respects. They all felt what it was like when Jesus showed up in the bars while He was on Earth.

Proverbs 25:11

GRACE NEVER FAILS

We can work harder, more creatively, and more diligently under grace than by any other means.

Still, some of us walk with only one foot in grace because we're afraid of what others will do with grace. We're afraid of what *we* will do with it! If someone wants to take advantage of grace, that's on them. Grace has not failed. Some people choose to trust grace and then fail. Then those who do not like the idea of grace blame it: "See, watch that grace stuff or people will try to get away with everything." They forget that we are new creatures, made to work best *only* under the motivation of grace.

You'll never work as hard or as sacrificially as you will under grace. An environment of grace takes away clock-watching compliance and replaces it with a motivation stronger than ought. Love becomes your purpose, your labor. It's God's secret to healthy companies, families, communities and ministries. So, wherever God has given us authority, it's worth walking in grace with both feet.

Acts 6:8

BIG DREAMING

God gives dreams. Huge dreams. Dreams bigger and better than you can conjure on your own. He wants your life to count. He didn't place you on Earth to play it safe, living to not make mistakes. Even friends and family may fear your taking God-sized risks, thinking they're protecting you from danger, even disappointment with God.

This doesn't mean you'll accomplish the visibly spectacular. Much of what is spectacular to God is relatively private and small. But He has something intentional for each of us. And His dreams for you are always more significant than your goals and more important than the sacrifices He calls you to. Ask God what He's dreaming for you. He loves to answer that prayer.

Also, invite trusted friends and family to suspend their anxiety for you long enough to tell you what they see. They carry the Spirit of God and can often wisely confirm what God's speaking to your heart.

You may be given dreams, new dreams, and dreams formed of failure. Either way, dream on.

Ephesians 3:20-21

NOT A COMMAND
TO BE SINLESS

The story of the woman caught in adultery ends with a jarring statement that seems to teach we should all stop sinning so much. In John 8:11 Jesus tells her, "Go and sin no more." It seems to say, "Look, I can't keep doing this for you. You've just got to stop sinning!"

Not at all. It's not in keeping with the consistent teaching of the New Testament.

Jesus is the one requesting this. He will die and rise from the dead for her. He will give her new life, a new way of how she can stop being owned by sin.

This is not a command for Mary to be perfect but an invitation to allow the perfect One to keep her from sinning. In full context, Jesus says, "I've forgiven you. I don't condemn you. Now you don't have to keep sinning the way you have. In trusting your relationship with Me, you have the ability to sin less."

John 8:1-11

YOU'RE A GRANDPARENT

You're a grandparent. You're excited and grateful to God. But that endorphin thing? It hasn't yet happened for you. You're embarrassed to tell anyone. Other grandparents slap you on the back and exclaim, "Aren't those little critters the best thing that's ever happened? Parents take 'em home at the end of the day! Go figure. Can't get enough of 'em, I tell ya." Hmmm. You really seem to be able to get enough of them.

Here's what you can do: Pick them up and sing songs for them about God and family. Even if you can't sing, they'll stare at you like you're Pavarotti. They may not remember the song, but they'll remember the love in your voice. You can ask them questions about their life, what's the most fun thing for them to do, what they like about their mom and dad, what they hope they can be when they grow up. Some of their ideas you can actually end up doing with them. Don't worry about those you can't. Eventually, you won't be able to get enough of 'em.

Proverbs 17:6

GRACE ALLOWS GLIMPSES

My friend,

I do not stop all pain or loss. I do not give less pain to better people. I know many might want this to be true, but it isn't. At so many funerals I hear, "How could God let this happen? He was so young, such a good person." Sometimes even those who know Me say this.

For people to come to me on the basis of faith and not prosperity, this reality will be played out in this way a little longer. The rain will continue to fall for a while longer on the just and the unjust. But grace allows you glimpses of what I'm doing in the middle of the unthinkable. I do not stop all pain or loss. But like new capillaries formed while training at high altitude, I am increasing your capacity to receive love. So, as great as the pain may be, it does not define you. My love does.

I know this is hard. But I am asking you to trust Me.

God

Philippians 3:7-11

FEAR

You've known it all your life. It can wake you up in the middle of the night and sweep over your entire being. It can be about money, the future, or your ultimate inability to protect the child in the next room. You might feel better once the sun rises. But fear can crouch there, in the back of your heart, just waiting to pounce again.

Long ago one person chose to feel and enter into fear itself, even though you could never experience or imagine it. Couldn't He have saved mankind without going through such intimate horror? Apparently His love chose not to do so.

The resurrected Christ offers words such as these: "My child, I know life will make you afraid—sometimes very afraid. But only remember this: I've overcome even death. So, what can the world or people do to you? I am your protection. I am Jesus."

John 14:27

SLEEP IN

Grace creates, for example, the ability to take a break and not feel guilty.

Now shame says, "You've no business messing around, letting tension off the bow. Next thing you know you'll be taking extra soy sauce packets at the food court. Get back to work. Skyscrapers don't build themselves while you're bowling."

But grace says, "Jesus knows your heart. When you need a break, take one. You give Him a good name when people around you are not uptight."

So go ahead, sleep in some morning. Clear your calendar and go fishing in the middle of the week. Schedule a pedicure *and* a manicure this week.

You may freely enjoy yourself playing hooky with the same sense of value as you would working overtime. God enjoys you equally in both settings.

Even if you overdo playing hooky, it won't be for long. You have a new heart that doesn't want to get away with anything.

People thrive under grace more than any other means.

Hit the snooze button. Or watch another episode of that cooking show!

Galatians 5:1

THE DANCE OF DOUBT AND FAITH

Some of us grew up in church circles where faith and doubt were pitted against one another. They were adversaries in a battle royale where there could be only one winner. But at some beautiful point along the way, God's grace swept us completely off our feet and we began to grow up, so to speak. And in so doing, we became men and women who began to put away some of those childish mindsets, the faith vs. doubt battle being one.

The writer Frederick Buechner once wrote: "Doubt is the ants in the pants of faith." In other words, a little doubt of the right variety keeps things moving, alive, maybe even hopping and dancing around. That's a wonderful way to think about doubt. The "childish" doubt had to do with questioning God's goodness, maybe even at times His existence. A more "mature" doubt has to do with questioning the limits we often put on how God might accomplish His good will in our lives.

God loves to surprise us, to keep us wide-eyed. And maybe keep us dancing.

1 Corinthians 2:9

9.29

GOLF

Like few other endeavors, golf can make you feel like a bad human being. After enough poor shots, you're certain the friends in your foursome are reconsidering their relationship with you.

Then you begin to behave like the unethical heathen you think you are. You make excuses; you talk rudely to the ball; you blame your clubs. You're tempted to improve the lie of your ball. Your scorecard becomes a record of what you can admit to and still face your family. Even God, you imagine, has had enough of you. "Oh come on! Keep your head down. Is that so hard? How am I to convince people I'm real when I can't even get the ball in flight?"

Demeaning words are never from Him, even when playing golf. So take a moment from behind the tree you just hit into and hear, "How I enjoy you! No game gets to define you. Nothing's changed with us. However, you might want to place the ball a little farther back in your stance."

John 10:27-28

OCTOBER

"Communities of grace and trust help us discover and define who we are and how we shall live in trust, love, grace, humility, dignity, and justice."
                                          -The Kingdom Life

BEAUTIFUL QUESTIONS

Learning who we are in Christ not only frees us from shame but also helps us discover what we get to do!

Then we help others discover what they're freed from and the wonder they've been freed into!

When I am no longer fighting to prove I'm enough, or hiding the things I fear will confirm I'm not enough, such beautiful questions emerge:

"God, who do I get to love?"

"God, who has been waiting to love me well?"

"God, how can I receive Your love, wildly and endlessly?"

"God, how do I best get to love those who don't know You?"

"God, what dreams and destinies are You forming in my heart?"

"God, what would You have for me to do with my life?"

"God, who can help me to mature into my destiny?"

"God, who can I help to mature into their destiny?"

"God, what do we do best together?"

Romans 11:33-36

PROMOTING CREATIVITY

Grace promotes a freedom to fail which can release immense success in a business or mission. Former Chairman and CEO of Service-Master, Bill Pollard believed, "In the absence of grace there will be no reaching for potential."

When I'm afraid I will pay for any failure, I tend to think concretely. I'll do only what is asked. When I am urged to risk, I'll try complex ways of solving a problem. If I'm not afraid to fail quickly, then I will seek to creatively and boldly find an answer. I have a tendency to think thoughts like, *These people seem to think that, given enough time and opportunity, I'm going to help come up with a solution to help this place flourish. Well, I'm going to try to prove them right.*

The atmosphere gets inspired and imaginative. We look forward to getting back to a conundrum, knowing we'll be honored for both breakthroughs and temporary setbacks.

Jesus taught this in the parable of the talents. He applauded those willing to take a faith-filled risk. In fact, He said, "Well done."

Matthew 25:14-30

JOY COMES IN THE MORNING

This is for all of us who tried out a life we thought would display our convictions of Christ's love, grace, life, freedom, healing and goodness.

And yeah, then that didn't quite play out.

Our own failure, or stuff that just came out of left field, ran like a brush fire through the world we naively thought was unassailable. We sat devastated amid the rubble, scarred.

And we're all gamely trying to find our way in the aftermath of disillusionment.

The vindication of trusting God is not proven or disproven in any accolade or advancement. It is not invalidated by career setback or the deterioration of strengths we thought we'd always have. It is found in what God does next, as we continue to stay close to Him in the daily playing out of this new reality.

The scars: They give you permission to influence even more than you imagined.

Joy will come, one of these mornings. Rest. He knows right where you are, and He adores you more than ten million yet-unnamed galaxies.

Psalm 30:4-5,11-12

WEARINESS

One of the cruelest effects of unremitting weariness is that it makes you forget. You become unable to remember much of the good God has done through you. Weariness is a dangerous place. Cynicism and disinterested self-protection are only blocks away.

How did this happen? Somewhere you may have been taught that ongoing weariness was a virtue, proof you were doing sacrificial stuff for God.

Get this: In Galatians 6:9, Paul encourages us to "not lose heart in doing good." And then he warns, "for in time we will reap if we do not grow weary."

And there it is. Weariness may be someone's virtue, but it's not God's.

Grace says we are not tools or machines for a God who is never happy unless we are exhausted and depleted. That's horrible theology.

It would be wise today to find time to be with those who can remind you of the good God has done through your life. These are friends who will help you remember that you were not born for utility but for beauty.

Isaiah 40:28-31

CALL IT OUT

We have encountered strong personalities who lead through intimidation. They controlled others by pointing out flaws and appointing themselves their spiritual doctor. We have also seen the destruction from the other side–communities that are too scared to say the hard things because it might not sound like grace. Two sides of the same unsafe coin.

Proverbs 27:6 says, "faithful are the wounds of a friend, profuse are the kisses of an enemy." One of the most beautiful gifts we can give a friend is the risk of calling them back to their true heart. When we desire to see them freed from the enemy's carefully crafted deception, we risk telling them hard things.

This is why it's so important to earn the earnest trust of your friends and family. In moments like these they are going to need to believe you love them. They might not like you a whole lot for a few moments, but they may just see your love more powerfully for this hard work of love.

Proverbs 27:6

HIS NAME IS JESUS

If you woke up today carrying self-doubt, self-disgust, or regret, you're not an exception. You're human—flesh and blood shocked at the newest revelation of pain, hurt and loss.

Our first response is rarely faith. It's usually about our failure or being failed. This time just call His name: Jesus. Then wait. Believe He's standing on your behalf, delighted to protect you. He has the ability to stop whatever's been started or to bring you peace in its continuing. Imagine Peter in that boat, knee deep in water, staring at Jesus after He stopped that killer storm. Jesus slowly breaks into a smile. Peter, drenched and undone, thinks, *All I've ever hoped for is transcended by this Man. He's brought an entirely new meaning to everything.* Never did a boat carry humans at such peace.

Nothing is irreparably wrong with you, friend. You're human. The stuffing comes out and the bolts loosen over time—no self-reform and no bold promises needed. Only His name. He is the One who holds you together. His name is Jesus.

Mark 4:35-41

OUR DEAR GOD

Every now and then it catches us off-guard. We find ourselves placed into the scene of heaven—not necessarily because we are more fervent or diligent in prayer.

But just because You make it so.

Maybe we are praying for one who is dying, repeating prayer-like words, when suddenly—*whoosh!*—we are *there*. Transported somehow. Even if we are imagining it from what we have read and heard. Regardless, You use it. And we are overwhelmed, undone, and absolutely no longer repeating prayer-like words.

We can see it. Almost everything. Like a glimpse of what we will see on *that* day.

It may be only moments, but it is enough to not only renew but also to stun our faith. It is more than enough to receive even a side-glance into the land whose God has it all figured out and is all complete.

Maybe it catches us off-guard in tears. Thank You, our dear God.

Revelation 21

TOGETHER PEOPLE

You don't have to live long on this planet to come to the conclusion that some people have it together and some don't. But that thought needs to be critically challenged, because it sets up a lie that can convince us we don't match up.

Geniality, gentility, and poise—they are mostly all beautiful and helpful. But even the most well-taught poise is an add-on. Under enough pressure, misfortune, and pain, it will break down.

Sometimes spectacularly.

There are no together people—only us, and we are as changed as we are ever going to be. We still are maturing. All this may or may not issue in gentility or impressive poise, but whatever has happened in us will hold up under pressure and misfortune—not always as a first response, but usually sometime thereafter. While sometimes messy, who we are does not usually intimidate others. It more often draws and convinces them that they too can live this redemptive life in Christ.

Look at you, all together and everything!

2 Corinthians 12:9-10

AFTER THE HONEYMOON

This grace awakening turned some of us absolutely upside down. It was like being born again, again. We tried to tell everyone we knew to read the books and listen to the music that had affected us so radically. We talked to them about passages from John, Romans, Galatians, Ephesians, Philippians, and much more scripture. But the reception was just sorta polite.

Eventually, we began to wonder if we had misunderstood something about this gospel of grace. Was it even accomplishing for us and our families and workplaces what we originally thought it would? Moralism at least gave us a list of to-dos to check off. Was this gospel going to hold up for us or was it an illusion?

Living in freedom is an art. Give yourself time to live into it. Eventually, you'll feel more convinced that you're not holding onto Jesus. He's holding onto you. Take heart. Watch the ones who've long risked this way of life. After the honeymoon comes the settling down into this grace, the building of a new life.

Galatians 5:1-13

SAY NO TO INTIMIDATION

Being "awed by" is an accurate response to one who is incredibly good at what you aspire to do. Sitting next to the current world-champion spoon thrower can feel overwhelming if spoon throwing happens to be your avocation.

Intimidation is different. It means to be "overawed," feeling unreasonably compelled to do what the other wants. Intimidation is unhealthy, practiced by those who coerce using force or threats. Most World Federation wrestlers employ it. So do unethical politicians.

God never wants you to experience such intimidation. The truths of who God says you are can free you from this ugliness.

However, just because you're feeling intimidated doesn't mean someone is trying to intimidate you. Insecurity can cause you to feel intimidated, even when it is not being attempted. Trusted friends can help clarify the accuracy of what you're feeling.

These words can put bona fide intimidation on the run: The God of the universe sees no inadequacy in me.

Except perhaps in spoon throwing.

1 Timothy 4:12

SIN WILL NOT BE MASTER OVER YOU

In Romans 6:14, Paul claims that sin shall not be master over you for you're no longer under Law but under grace. No joke. If you choose to come under grace, sin will not dominate you like it did before.

It's also a warning.

If you choose to not submit under grace, sin will deceive you and cause you to hide. It'll remain master over you, in one insidious form or another. We must expose the misconstrued verses given to you by usually well-intentioned people. Behavior management can dress you up and sanitize your appearances, but it doesn't lead to the freedom for which Christ set you free.

Freedom comes only by trusting Christ's redemptive work, trusting others, and trusting who He says you are. Only grace can get you to think about something other than your sin.

Well lived, lovers of grace. Well lived.

Romans 6:1-4

FINDING EACH OTHER IN THIS GRACE (PART ONE)

From all ages, ethnicities, and orientations, all socio-economic and educational levels, you're finding each other under this banner of grace. It is a growing family, finding each other virtually and actually. It's wildly encouraging to watch.

Many of you are angry. You feel betrayed by the institutional church, by your parents, pastors, authors—and even yourselves. Some are angry it took this long to discover the authentic gospel they should have grown up on. Many have given up on anything resembling a local church, doubtful it is possible for grace to exist in one. You have reasons to be angry and mistrusting. *But you can't just stay there.* The trouble with mistrust is that it will metastasize, spreading into your entire way of life.

Feel your anger deeply. Don't move away from it prematurely. But know you can't stay there. Trust is absolutely essential to the life of grace and to this beautiful family, of which you are now a member.

1 Peter 1:22

FINDING EACH OTHER IN THIS GRACE (PART TWO)

"I grew up in the church and all we ever got was moralizing sermons of how bad we were. Where was this message of grace?" It's enough to make you scream. But ultimately, anger never wins anything. It eventually makes you too much like those whose clouded theology you've run from. You can become someone more focused on what you're against while forgetting what you're *for*. And you wake up one day to find yourself smug, judgmental, superior, and too cool for everyone else. This is most certainly not grace.

Grace is so much better than smugness. Grace gradually makes you feel more alive, playful, true, authentic, safe, available, sacrificial and honest. Mostly, it makes you free to live for the sake of loving others. If grace is to make a difference in the theological culture, it is imperative that we find ourselves intent on loving others more fully and leaving what we are against to the peddlers of the hazy theology we've walked away from.

Luke 6:35

FINDING EACH OTHER IN THIS GRACE (PART THREE)

For those of us who hold these truths of grace, there's a caveat. We can turn grace into a theological concept to be "right" about rather than a life shared with others. We can talk about grace correctly and still not enjoy the grace we're talking about. We end up simply switching one head theology for another, turning this beautiful grace into another system of law, complete with a prescribed set of "grace rules" and buzz words. C'mon, there's no secret handshake to grace. It'll look different in every culture. Everyone matures at their own rate.

This is a beautiful season in history where prisoners of moralism are reaching the point where they can't do it anymore. They are asking questions. They want to reread the scriptures without a lens of moralism. Those of us who love, while still confronting failure, immaturity, and clumsiness, have a precious opportunity to take them by the hand into freedom. Let's make sure what they find is more genuine than what they left.

Galatians 5:13-14

I KNOW WHO I AM

A fellow legislator was sitting with Senator Tom Coburn from Oklahoma. He said, "Tom, over your years in the House and the Senate you have sometimes frustrated voters and fellow senators alike on both sides of the aisle. Your positions often did not follow party lines. You voted your conscience. You are respected and loved, but what you did was often unpopular. I'm sure it was hard. I just wanted to thank you and ask how you did it." Tom thought for a bit and then answered, "I have only been able to do what you say because I know who I am, and whose I am."

Looking back, we're probably aware that any courageous and unpopular choice we have made comes from the same place of confidence and conviction of believing to whom we belong. Knowing who we are allows us to transcend the glow of popular opinion and the tide of moral expediency. At the end we'll say, "I have only been able to do what I've done because I trust who God says I am."

2 Timothy 1:12-14

DAY-DREAMING OF GLORY

There is a broken world system not of God. It booms loudly in the background, constantly attempting to preoccupy your every thought. Like a drill sergeant, it shouts in your subconscious that you're hopelessly behind and will never catch up.

Even relaxed, you know you're on call. You end up self-protecting in fear by churning and keeping dutifully on task.

But you can rebel against the machine. Anytime. Anywhere.

You must first courageously contend that the shouting voices are never God's voice.

Then you can imagine Home—where you will one day meet the God who thinks you are more than enough. Give it a dangerously expensive few moments and He may become overpoweringly visible. You can practice imagining the moment you'll first see Him face to face.

Each time you do, you mock the belching system trying to run you. Each time you shout, "I know who I am and how this finishes," you muffle the drill sergeant a little more.

The world's system cowers at such day-dreaming of glory.

Colossians 3:1-4

RETURNED INNOCENCE

One of the most astonishing realities of our relationship with Jesus is that we are able to be clean and blameless before Him at any moment, no matter what we've done! Even saying that seems wrong, like we can get away with something, even a terrible thing, in the wink of a prayer. But there it is—sin paid for in total, ready to be believed and applied to your situation.

In fact, daring to receive your blamelessness empowers you to not stay in or return to the sin you just repented of. There may be amends to make and consequences to absorb for your choices, but wallowing in your failure should not be one of them.

Consider an issue where you've previously been stuck in guilt and shame. You may walk out into the light of this day as clean as the just-purchased shirt you pulled off its hanger. Cleanness. Blamelessness. Returned innocence. One of the most exhilarating experiences on the planet.

Ephesians 1:3-4

SITTING WITH JESUS

You're weary, but you're here now, unhurried, sitting with Jesus. So what can you expect to happen?

Maybe you'll first feel time slow down. You might hear your own heart beating. Then an involuntary sigh. Then what? Invitation. You're free to get things out, to sing if you want to. There's no right or wrong place to wander. Release emotions you've been holding in. Even ask questions you once would've been afraid to utter. Then quiet. You feel you should bring up your stuff; the failures and compromises. That familiar drill.

But then there's Jesus. You sense He is smiling in kind, lighthearted, knowing delight. You smile too. You're drawn to replay when you first remember trusting His love, when you first felt His absolute affection. You reach out your hands, needing to express what words cannot contain. Then the phone rings. The scene dissolves. This interaction is over.

It's not always like this. But sometimes, sitting with Jesus is much like this.

1 John 4:18-19

BEING LOVED

Some have figured out how to sacrificially love significant others in their lives. That's profoundly important. Many never figure this out. But, even if you do, it's not enough. Each of those you're sacrificially loving carries an innate longing and need from God to sacrificially love you!

Few things are as painful, over time, as not being let in to meet needs in the life of someone they love. They can see you pretty accurately—usually the more love, the more accuracy. It's hard to watch you struggle without permission to protect you. Their joy comes in getting to love you in your worst stuff.

If this devotional describes you, then you get to love better than ever before by letting trusted others actively care for you. It might begin by telling them you'd like to give them permission to address an area where they see you struggle. Let them. It won't be easy at first. But soon it will feel like discovering new hope.

Being loved is what lovers get to experience.

John 13:34-35

NEVER DESIGNED TO BLUFF

"Am I a phony, a con, getting by on manufactured confidence and bluffing?" Every assignment or project with a deadline threatens to expose you as a fraud for all to see. This fear of failure can cause you to fail or push you to thrive—but thriving in the misery of doubt and self-loathing.

It is a great freedom to know God is really good with your capacity, or lack of it. He created you intentionally. No failure can define you. You are infinitely more than your job. So if He is good with who you are, then failure no longer has the same power. In fact, failure can expose what you can do best. You will still work hard but without the self-doubt

God believes the real you is not a phony, even as you are still trying to pretend. He can see through to the real you, not to condemn, but to call you to freedom.

Galatians 5:1

LISTENING BEFORE DEFENDING

Is there anything harder than, in the middle of a heated discussion, choosing to listen before giving your next point? If you don't reload with an objection while the other is talking, you're going to lose the argument. And if you lose the argument, you might lose your place at the table. And respect. And a chance at being listened to seriously in the next interaction. Maybe its deeper. The fear may be that you're not enough. If only you could finally be right on an issue, then all would see.

No win will ever accomplish or take away so much. But the moment you give yourself permission to listen, you're proving you trust God can take care of your reputation as you choose to do what is right. You're offering respect to the other and reminding them there's something higher at stake than a win. Suddenly the argument becomes a safe place to learn. Everyone in the room realizes something sacred is taking place.

Proverbs 25:12

SEASONS

God created the earth with seasons. One follows another, like clock-work. Seasons are predictable, inevitable, both comforting and satis-fying. Nobody gets to go sledding in a world where it's always spring.

Apparently, God created you and me with seasons too. There are not four of them, and they don't repeat exactly throughout our lives. But they definitely move us along. This is deeply encouraging. No-body would get to know what redemption feels like in a life with only laughter. Plus, it's deeply hopeful to know that we won't always be in our present condition. In other words, this too shall pass.

It can be uncomfortable to move from one season to the next. But it is more painful to try to stay in a season from which God is nudging you forward. You don't usually have to figure out why. God is the one who changes seasons. You just get to gradually, clumsily, sense it's happening—then try not to fight it.

Acts 14:17

LOVING STRANGERS (PART ONE)

Say you plan a day off where you try this. No kids or spouse—just you. At least this first time. Just you and God driving around, loving folk. Go at your own pace, for as long as you'd like. This is gonna be fun.

Maybe you ask the person behind you in line at a coffee shop if they'd be alright with you paying for their order. (Make sure they're not ordering for a soccer team.) You might say, "I felt like God would like me to do this for you." Or don't put the *God* part in. God's able to let them know you're with Him if He wants.

If a conversation starts, just be you. Don't force something no one's asking. Your only goal is for the other to feel valued. When they get home, they might say, "Hey, this person standing in line bought my coffee. It was so cool. I want to do that for someone."

Well played. Now, where are you going next?

Hebrews 13:1-2

LOVING STRANGERS (PART TWO)

Yep, just you and God, driving around, loving folk. So, where to next?

Maybe you're now on public transit. Deep breath. Sit down next to someone. You could share something you're struggling with. Staring straight ahead, you could say, "You ever have one of those days where it all breaks down? I had one recently." If they don't get up, they may eventually respond, "Yeah?" That's enough to tell a bit of your story. Just story, no solutions. Nobody was asking for solutions. At some point they might say, "Yeah, I struggle too sometimes. Not like *your* stuff, but . . ." You can endure the awkward silence. They may offer the great gift of letting you in, to tell you their pain.

Many go years without the chance to get that out. If the ride is long enough, one occasionally risks, "So, what do you do? You know, like when it gets so bad you wanna run?" Easy now. No answers. Only identification. Maybe share some of the hope within you. You two just met.

1 Peter 3:15

GOOD NEWS ABOUT DESIRE

If we explore research on pornography and cohabitation, like that by Regenrus & Ueckers or Meg Jay, we'll discover the devastating downside of sex outside marriage. These data assess the results of a sexual relationship based on consumerism; that is buying a good, until the good no longer satisfies, which requires the next search for an enhanced product. Empirical data confirms what you hunch—consumer sex is overwhelmingly demoralizing and disintegrating.

The dominant faith-based approach to this issue has been "lust management." Clearly, this approach fails mightily.

Groundbreaking researcher, Jay Stringer, signals God's true design for resolving unwanted sexual desire when he says, "addressing sexual struggles through the lens of abhorrent behavior intensifies shame, and shame drives us deeper into the very behavior we wish to stop." Pardoxical, isn't it? Until we realize God's solution all along was to die and pay for *both* our sin and shame. Christ gave us a shame-free identity, so we could actually face our shame-based behaviors, and begin the hard and freeing work of journeying toward sexual wholeness.

Isaiah 61:3

STAY CURIOUS, MY FRIENDS

A mature dose of doubt in your faith is good for your health. It can go a long way in keeping you a student of life and people for life. Yet far too many Christians reach a stage in life when they think they've seen and heard it all. So they essentially lock the door to their minds and prevent anything new from knocking and possibly coming in.

There's a very descriptive word for this kind of living: close-minded.

However, there is an alternative: living open-minded, being Curious with a capital C. Such people are easy to pick out in crowds if you'll listen because they're always saying things like, "You know, I never thought about it that way before," or the wonderful old standard, "Well, I'll be."

That's right, curiosity can keep you young at heart. Just think, if you stay curious over the course of your life right up until the point where you step across into that next place that Jesus has been preparing just for you, then your last/first words might be, "Now this, this is something else."

John 14:5-13

EARNING THE
TRUST OF OUR KIDS

Earning trust is not an ethereal exercise. As parents or mentors, we want to influence those we care for. We want to impart the best of who we are. But nothing kicks in until we're trusted by them. Children who know their parents are winnable, thoughtful, and walking in integrity are vitally influenced by them.

Once they know that we can be trusted, we get to offer them three astonishing things: love, truth, and guidance.

We didn't get this privilege by powering up, demanding respect, or guilting them into obedience. That only ever gains disrespect, mistrust and hiding.

It's telling them what you can and cannot be trusted to do. It's being honest when you fail. It's not using your role to win. This takes the contentiousness out of parenting. There will still be conflict, hard choices, times of withdrawal. But underlying everything will be a trust that will keep their hearts soft and winnable for a lifetime.

1 Thessalonians 1:5-6

IF THEY'RE
STILL WATCHING
(PART ONE)

We say that the world's still watching us and the result of our faith. With all respect, we may be flattering ourselves. Many may be past watching or are watching now to mock. If they are still watching, or listening, they are completely disinterested in our preaching, our threats of hell, our political convictions, our moral stands, our positions on marijuana, abortion, gun control, premarital sex, to name a few.

Somewhere in the last half of the twentieth century, the Church lost some of her voice. Religion became irrelevant for a large audience. They tuned us out. The pietistic anger, the insider language, the self-congratulatory tone—they stopped listening. If we are to regain our voice, we will have to change our voice—not the message, but the approach. The conviction that the disbelieving simply need to hear our right way and then they will come to Jesus needs to be rethought. We can show them a Jesus different from the one they've relegated to holidays or rejected altogether.

Acts 1:8

IF THEY'RE
STILL WATCHING
(PART TWO)

So, how are we to speak to our disbelieving or often disillusioned friends, if many of them have relegated us to the edge of town? How do we reach those who are politely dismissive and others who aggressively attack faith in Jesus?

Instead of demanding that they come to us, we may need to go to them. It may need to be from as close up as Jesus engaged humanity. The crowds in His day had watched shell games and fake messiahs. So Jesus went directly to them. He went to where people congregated who could not kid themselves about needing a doctor. We too can show up that close, offering only the person of Jesus. We carry Him. God can cause them to see Jesus in us. The message won't change, but the delivery system will. We approach in humility, no longer presuming they're predisposed to want what we are offering. This may be a marvelous new day of close-up conversations, where we listen as much as we speak.

Luke 19:1-10

BEING KNOWN TO OUR KIDS (PART ONE)

We fear that if we tell our kids about the wrong choices of our past, it will give them permission to make similar choices. If we buy into this thinking, we'll present an idealized person to them they'll never be able to live up to or trust. It will keep us from being known to our kids. When we remain unknown, we leave them alone in their decision making, vulnerable to repeating the same wrong choices we made.

But when you tell your story, age appropriately, to your kids, you teach your evaluation of the consequences of your choices. You get to be the one who tells them what really happened and how it affected you and others. You're protecting them by giving them an example of what they're facing right now, but with your evaluation of the consequences. Your vulnerability will earn trust from their hearts. They'll come to trust you to protect them in what they struggle with. There may be no more wonderful gift for a parent to give.

1 Thessalonians 2:7-8

BEING KNOWN TO OUR KIDS (PART TWO)

Once you've decided that you want to be more known by your kids, all sorts of questions surface: What do they need to know? What do they *want* to know? How would you bring any of this up?

Maybe go for a drive with your oldest. Imagine what stories from your past could possibly relate to what they might be going through or might someday go through. "Would you like to hear about the time I got locked in the trunk of my parents' car?" "About when my family moved to a new town?" "The time my first boyfriend broke up with me?" "The time I failed geometry?" "The time I got drunk at a party?" You get to laugh at yourself and recall your assessment then and now: what you wish you could do over and why.

There's no sermon—just two humans finding each other. It may be awkward. They may not want to hear your stories. Eventually they will. They want to know you.

1 Corinthians 13:11-12; Philippians 4:18

"I need to start believing who God says I am and live from that."

-Bo's Cafe

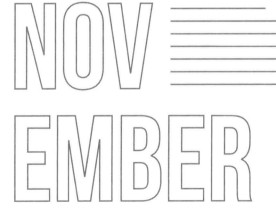

A STAR WITNESS

Due to our own quite-compromised lives, many of us are afraid to tell others with confidence about Jesus.

Yet, you are a star witness. You may reason, "Once I've cleaned up my act, then I will proudly say, 'Hey look at what Jesus can do!'"

Look, the strength of your testimony is not about your superior behavior. No one comes to trust Jesus because of your improved behavior. Your evidence is that God has given you a new heart and an increasingly freeing journey, which includes your failures and actual present-tense sin—that is, how He loves you, enjoys you, protects you, walks with you, reveals you to you, calls you out, and completely forgives you in the midst of all of it.

God can handle your immaturity and the truth of what you really do. Allow yourself to be a star witness to the stunning wonder of who He really is—even if in telling it you later discover you had green-chili salsa stains on your sleeve and were wearing mismatched socks.

Romans 8:15

DID JESUS LAUGH?

Because we can't find direct verses showing Jesus laughing or smiling, it can render this whole humor thing a bit suspect. To some the spiritual life is quiet and somber. When they enter a house of worship, they want it *respectfully silent*.

Totally get it. But what if laughter is some of the best worship that can be offered?

Though we've no biblical record that Jesus sighed, we're still pretty sure He did. If certain situations cause an involuntary reaction to joyful laughter, *we can safely assume God created the function*. We can be equally confident Jesus laughed. And often.

Many events and thoughts are hilarious to those who love Jesus. That evening at the wedding in Cana, after the disciples got over the shock, there must have been laughter. Probably only the disciples, Jesus, His mom and some very happy waiters were in on the miracle. Watching happy wedding-goers dancing and discussing the wine that must have tasted better than a 1962 Domaine de la Romanee-Conti—it's hard to not bust a gut at that.

Psalm 126:1-3

WHAT YOU UNIQUELY CAN GIVE

Right now in your world, someone is dramatically in need of what you have. Much of the time they have received trite or religiously oversimplified answers. It has done more damage than good. They are drowning in clichés. The answers they've been given do not fit with their unrelenting grief. They don't even know yet that they need what you have. They've lost their capacity to keep trying something new. They're lost.

But then you show up. You're tempered by your own long season of easy answers that didn't help. You won't say much because you're not yet sure what they need. You'll impress upon them that they matter and that their God is in the center of this with them. You know that much is true. You tell them so. Because you are wary of potentially careless words, they'll trust what you say.

When you leave, they will have an altered hope, different from the minute before you arrived. They called out to God for help, for someone just like you.

2 Corinthians 1:1-11

CHRISTIANITY AND POLITICS

Speaking about C. S. Lewis, Philip Yancey said that Lewis "observed that almost all crimes of Christian history have come about when religion is confused with politics. Politics, which always runs by the rules of ungrace, allures us to trade away grace for power, a temptation the church has often been unable to resist."

Much goodness is done in the political arena. Legislation can relieve a country's famine, or provide financial stability or healthcare to many.

But politics is run by power. And absolute power absolutely corrupts.

We're called to honor and pray for our leaders. But Christ's power and authority are revealed by the Church. When we believe politics can somehow legislate Christian goodness, all manner of madness is poured into patriotism and faith.

The Church gets played as if Jesus is relegated to conservative or liberal. He is neither. At our core, neither are we. We belong to the Kingdom.

Have a good day, fellow citizen.

Philippians 3:20

THE GRACE PARTY

There is a well-grooved belief that we must take a stand on every political issue of the day. And our friends must conform to our beliefs if we are to be truly friends. News anchors and commentators define who our enemies must be. Gradually our world shrinks to the size of a political ideology.

Grace gives a different story. It gives us permission to actively love those diametrically opposed to our positions, without agreeing to their positions. Grace enlarges our world and takes on the suffering of those harmed by dishonorable decisions.

We who have chosen to follow Jesus are part of a third way. We are identified neither as liberal nor as conservative. Our political positions are too small a thing to separate us. The scriptures are pretty clear that the message of the gospel and the message of political structures rarely have the same ultimate goal, regardless of which flag they are waving.

In a sense, Christ-followers are to always vote third party—the grace party.

Galatians 3:28

RECEIVING CRITIQUE

Even if you've asked for it, the assessment of how you're doing on a project or in a relationship can feel too close, too much. Something as small as a negative assessment of a flower on your canvas can convince you your entire painting is a disaster. You find yourself gradually asking fewer and fewer people to give critique until finally almost no one can challenge any area of your work—or even the color of your pants.

One of the surpassing gifts of grace is the confidence to be less afraid of critique. Grace convinces you to believe you are enough already and proves it with specific examples. Grace says you won't be ruined even if everyone's negative critique is accurate. Grace says you have endless value to God, before you try anything. So, everything you try is a bonus. If it happens to be appreciated, great! If not, great!

Proverbs 27:5-6

NO DISTINCTION

History carries the stench of despicable, extended seasons of systemic racism. Any race dominating and suppressing another is clear proof mankind is broken.

Shockingly, the Church has shared in the guilt. But we have also been, at times, the strongest voices of freedom from it.

Paul teaches us to "put on the new self who is being renewed to true knowledge according to the image of the One who created him—a renewal in which there is no distinction between Greek and Jew, circumcised and uncircumcised, barbarian, Scythian, slave and freeman, but Christ is all in all."

This teaching can change the world in our lifetime. We're free to see everyone made in the image of God. We're free to put on the "renewal" of believers, where our only distinction is Christ. We're free to fully love every human, believer or not. We're free to stand against any hint of elitism in the Church or in society.

When we model all this out, we get to show love overcomes hatred.

We get to show it is possible.

Colossians 3:9-11

SOMETHING MORE IMPORTANT

Many of us have played our hand on social media. We've been sucked into the arena of digitally detached debate. We've taken our stand on gun control, presidents, gender-appropriate bathrooms, J. Edger Hoover, Area 51, and the Trilateral Commission.

We may have also tried to create an environment of grace on our Facebook page—a place where it would be safe for everyone to show up. About every week we're tempted to disrupt that safety. We could say so much about everything swirling around us. A month rarely goes by when we're not chastised for not saying more about race relations, the White House, guns, North Korea, and a thousand other peccadillos.

There are times when it is important to speak truth in grace, but there is also a beautiful and powerful gift you can offer the conversation by staying out of it. We all need to see someone not taking the bait.

Relax. While it is important to have conversations that matter, you can point people to Jesus. He is the only one with the answers to our culture's mysteries.

Colossians 2:3

OUR DEAR GOD

God, sometimes we do not understand ourselves. We are tightly wound bundles of contradiction. We want to live for Your glory, and yet we're tripped up by vanity and pettiness. We know we are new creations but are shocked by our selfish actions. We make claims about Your life in us to non-believers, but at times they appear more Christ-like than us. We play games and wear masks, even as we accuse others of playing games and wearing masks. We major on minors and minor on majors. We often choose to not share Your love.

Yet, we hold to this unshakable reality. We are, each of us, intertwined with You! You live in us. We live in You. No matter how petulantly, indifferently, and flippantly we behave, we are immovable and unbreakable. We will ultimately glorify You and live out of Your life in us. This goodness that has taken over joyously befuddles us most of all.

Romans 7:14–8:4

LOVE ALWAYS TRUSTS

Some people say we have no obligation to trust others because the Bible never commands us to trust one another, only God. What would you say to these folks?

You may be encouraged to recall that in healthy relationships, "love always trusts" (1 Corinthians 13:7). Trust and love are inseparable. Without trust you cannot sustain love, which is the key mark of a Christ-follower.

Also, when one presumes that a verse must be found to confirm a truth (though we just quoted one), it's like presuming there is no Trinity because the word doesn't exist in the Bible.

Finally, imagine Jesus promoting this philosophy by saying to His disciples, "Boys, when I leave there will be no need for you to trust each other anymore, only God."

Imagine a world without trust and you've imagined a deceptive realm directed by the evil one. We were rescued from a world of untrustworthy lies into one built on trust, because this Kingdom is anchored in grace and truth.

Trust somebody with you today.

1 Corinthians 13:7

SIMPLE CHANGES

The workplace can be its own island of self-serving, fear-based, unhealthy driving forces. But simple changes can revolutionize your workplace.

This exercise can be used in hiring, reviews, and informal team relationships. We've seen it practically release the grace of Jesus into business and professional cultures. It's a basic but profound application of humility. Recall, humility attracts God's grace.

For example, when hiring, invite a supervisor to model to the potential employee how she has deferred to the strengths of one lower down in the organizational chart so that her weaknesses can be protected. This is to protect, not excuse, a weakness. It is acknowledging, "I don't do well in this category of relationship or skill, and I need your strength to do my best work." Invite the potential employee to interact with you on what they've just seen. It is profound how this one exercise in humility can revolutionize the hiring process and the current workplace area in which you serve.

In whatever capacity God has given, you can help foster grace in your culture.

2 Corinthians 9:8

TOO MUCH AFFIRMATION?

Some of us fear giving or receiving affirmation. We're concerned that the affirmed one will become arrogant, full of themselves. That way of seeing may betray a flawed theology. It says that affirmation, which is a form of being loved by another, triggers pride or conceit. But being loved through affirmation does not cause egotism or self-importance. It actually prompts gratitude and joy in you.

Affirmation helps to clarify your identity, reinforce your confidence, nurture your character, and even foster the healing of wounds. Honest affirmation also humbles you and causes you to want to do more of what you are being affirmed for.

What a wonderful way to live. Instead of bragging on ourselves or fawning for praise, God gives us a much more meaningful way. He designed you to be affirmed; it's a need He embedded in you that can only be met by God and others. So He says, "Let another praise you, and not your own mouth." Think about who you might affirm today.

Proverbs 27:2

A RUNNER'S SECRET

A seasoned high school runner gave this great counsel to an aspiring runner: "Pain is temporary. You have talent. But you're not allowing yourself to risk the pain necessary to succeed." This radically changed that younger runner's trajectory.

Watch any high school track meet and you'll without exception witness runners sprinting like mad the last hundred or so yards of a 5,000-meter race. They ran guardedly most of the laps. They realized too late they had much more to give, but they were afraid of shuffling in the last lap and being embarrassed in front of friends and family.

Peter gives perspective to runners in the faith. First Peter 5:10 says, "And the God of all grace . . . after you have suffered for a little while will Himself perfect, confirm, strengthen and establish you." He's saying, in essence, "Suffering for good in this race is temporary." Instead of guarding our hearts for fear of embarrassment, we run this race with courage, trusting that a good God is waiting at each milepost to strengthen us.

Jude 1:24-5

SHE IS NOT ALONE

Her crime is that she married poorly and stayed too long. Tonight she is driving two hundred miles to Palm Beach to move in with her parents until she can regroup. She looks back at her three-year-old son asleep in his car seat. Her husband was abusive and then unfaithful. In his manipulation he convinced her that their failed marriage was her fault. Now she's driving from a world where she can no longer live to a home she never wanted to return to. She will need to be brave for a thousand more evenings, to believe she is more than how he defined her.

She, or someone like her, will one day drive into your town. This story is playing out more and more. She is terrified to trust deeply again. She can bluff confidence but inside she is fighting to hold it together. Jesus is right there with her tonight. He is so proud of her. But she struggles mightily to dare believe that it is true.

This is where you come in.

1 Thessalonians 2:11

CONVICTIONS

Success is an interesting animal. It can make you opportunity-driven instead of conviction-driven. Then you're wide open to "succeeding" at becoming someone you never wanted to be!

Convictions, on the other hand, get formed away from applause, achievement, and followers. They are about who God has called you to be, what you want your life to be about, the influence you believe God wants you to have.

Convictions are also about who you *don't* want to be. You're deciding that your integrity will not be bought, that a larger stage must be the right stage. When you make choices from your convictions, you are deciding the nature of your significance and influence, what you'll pass on to your children and their children.

When you make choices from opportunity, the nature of your significance gets decided *for* you. A mature friend can help you sort through all this. Convictions can come at any age to radically affect the rest of your journey.

1 Thessalonians 5:11

UNRESOLVED STUFF

Most of us are awakening to the pain of realizing we can't control our lives the way we thought we could. We're stuck with unresolved issues whose symptoms we're trying to fix without the help of anyone else.

An unresolved issue is a recurring problem increasingly affecting your life that never seems to get any better. You know you're carrying around one (or more) when one or several key people tell you that you're overreacting to a situation. You can usually trace this back to one or more of three woundings: your own sin, someone's sin against you, or someone important to you consistently choosing to not love you.

Grace offers an environment powerful enough to resolve these historical patterns damaging your relationships. A resolved sin is not a "fixed sin"; rather, it is one that is being processed in an environment of light (grace). What if there was a place so safe that the worst of you could be known and you would discover that you would be loved more, not less, in the telling of it?

1 John 5:3-4

THE CROSS

It happened on our earth. Not in another galaxy, but in the same air we breathe. You can still feel the reverberations, as much as on the day after it happened. The cross of Jesus is always present tense. It's where love gave its most complete and vivid explanation. God is saying, "Everything you have become is because of what He did. What you know of goodness, faith, love, sacrifice, and bravery is based in that single event."

For it to matter, Jesus had to experience what it would be for a human to endure the depth and length of what we were to suffer. Even more, He had to *choose* it. It was not imposed upon Him. Jesus, in some way, said, "Father, I can see what this will cost. But I already know them. To bring them home to Us will be *full joy*. It is worth a universe more than whatever the evil one will form against Me." So the Trinity begins a timetable to save us from ourselves.

Matthew 27:46

SECRETS

In the riveting *Heart of Man* movie we learn the shattering consequences of unhealthy "secrets." Some secrets are meant to be kept. But, many secrets are meant to be shared. You cannot get healthy living with most secrets. In the film's After Show, Traylor Lovvorn quotes the famous slogan, "We're only as sick as our secrets."

This is highlighted by another quote from the film, "The best scenario I could see living in the dark was to keep everything a secret, because if I kept everything a secret, no one would get hurt."

Hording unhealthy secrets to keep yourself or others "safe" is one of the biggest lies you could believe. The more you believe in your immovable identity in Christ, the more you are free to share the unhealthy secrets you've been holding on to. Grace releases you to tell your secrets to a few trusted friends. Live free.

1 John 1:6-10

REPLACING YOUR OLD ABILITY

You gave up so many things when you gave your life over to Jesus—your right to self-protection, mask-wearing, blame, suck-it-up-and-take-it, self-justification, and self-vindication. You gave up willpower to fight sin.

That's right. You've forfeited the assumed power you once carried. When you revert to its meager strength, it's of less value than ever before. Religion without the experience of supernatural power is just guilt, failure, and self-loathing waiting to happen. It creates hypocrites and self-pious Pharisees, or defeated, cynical strivers.

But ours is a supernatural life, with the Holy Spirit living inside of us! He's fighting our fights, whether we think to ask Him or not. No matter what you've gotten yourself into, or what has happened to you, God's got you. First Peter 5:10 proclaims the replacement to your old power: "After you have suffered for a little while, the God of all grace, who called you to His eternal glory in Christ, will Himself perfect, confirm, strengthen and establish you."

1 Peter 5:10

THAT'S HOW

How does God explain that no one is an outcast with Him? Jesus heals a leper.

How does God explain that He does not condemn us? Jesus defends the prostitute from religious authorities.

How does God explain His humility? Jesus enters Earth as a baby.

How does God explain His love for the lost? Jesus eats with the tax collectors.

How does God explain His compassion? Jesus brings a father's daughter back from the dead.

How does God explain His specific, unique love for me? Jesus describes the shepherd searching for the one sheep.

How does God explain that He wrestles with our same temptations? Jesus suffers in the desert.

How does God explain that He enters into our deep pains? Jesus suffers in the garden.

How does God explain His tender affection for us? Jesus weeps and grieves over us.

How does God explain His sense of humor? Jesus turns water into wine.

How does God explain the nature of ultimate power? Jesus displays an empty tomb.

Hebrews 1:1-4

THE GOOD GOD AND SUFFERING

Suffering is largely a blanket term for the painful stuff that gets through. God does not stop all of the damaging effects of living on a fallen planet. One day He will. Completely. But not yet.

There is a suffering we experience because God, as a perfect, loving Father, will not allow us to continue to harm ourselves. Discipline is the loving correction a parent gives to bring their child back into the safety of who they really are. It is administered by a Father who loves us more than we know how to love ourselves. It's never punishment, for that imposes the will of the law or whoever has authority to even the score.

Of course, not all suffering is God's discipline. No one can accurately tell anyone why a particular suffering exists. So much suffering we experience has nothing to do with discipline. All we know is there's a God overseeing it all and using it to bring about supernatural goodness through drawing us back to who we really are.

Hebrews 12:1-17

A DAY IN THE LIFE

Today you are being offered a gift certificate. It's good for up to three months and then expires. You may sleep in as late as you want. You may get up, eat breakfast, read the paper, and then go back to sleep again if you like. You may wear pajamas all day long. You may eat cereal for breakfast, lunch, and dinner. You may binge watch all media. You may binge nap. You may read an entire book. You may listen to music as loud as you like while dancing around the house holding a bowl of ice cream. Or a bowl of chili.

"But I can't do that. I'm not being productive. I'm a drain on society." You're free to hold that theology 364 days of the year—but not today.

You may decline the offer. But why? Without it, you'll eventually be so drained you will be a drain on everyone who crosses your path. By the way, God cannot wait to spend this day with you. Enjoy the day.

Colossians 2:16-23

THE UMBRELLA MAN

You might run into Umbrella Man if you visit the historic district in downtown Hong Kong. He repairs umbrellas. Who does that? They're cheap and easily disposable. The first bent rib and you take it to the thrift store.

The Umbrella Man sees life differently. He presumes the umbrella could have been a gift from someone dear or was passed down from a treasured grandparent. He has taught many in Hong Kong to value their umbrella because of its potential attachment to a larger human story. Dignity is expressed from the lesser to the greater.

So it is with God. All things have their dignity and honor because He has attached them to a larger human story. And all humans have majestic dignity and honor because of their attachment to a larger God story. Look around you today. Beauty and dignity surround you. You can honor them. As Brother Lawrence said centuries ago, "It is enough for me to pick up a straw from the ground for the love of God." From the lesser to the greater.

Luke 12:27-28

AN ETERNAL SONG

There is a song that is uniquely yours with God. He's been singing it over you from before you were born and you'll sing it back to Him throughout eternity (see Revelation 5:9). It continues to be refreshed, with new lyrics (see Psalm 33:3). He personally places the words into your heart and mouth (see Psalm 40:3). He reminds you of the song at night, when you're afraid (see Job 35:10). You can sing as often as you'd like. He loves it. But this song sings when you can't, even in groans too deep for words. When you arrive Home, you'll hear it again. "There it is! He sang this over me. At times, I sang it back."

You may think that He wouldn't sing over you, with what you know about you. But would the God who created song forget to write one for you, the you He loves as much as anyone? Yeah, not a chance.

Yes, there are seasons when you can't hear, let alone sing. Maybe that's today. Maybe today is a day to simply hum your song in your heart.

Zephaniah 3:17

FINDING HIS OWN

On any particular morning in rural western Africa, a young girl is staring at the moon as she walks to collect water from a nearby town, overwhelmed at how big it looks in the clear night sky. Suddenly, this girl who has yet to hear anything about God, is calling out to Him: "Your sky is so beautiful. Who are you? I want to know You. Please talk to me."

There is no local pastor or Christian yet within reach of her life. But God will find her and save her, no more or less miraculously than anyone who comes to know Him. There are endless theological problems and questions around the issue of salvation; there probably always will be.

Early morning, somewhere in Togo, God hears one of His flock. He knows her voice.

Ecclesiastes 3:11

GO AHEAD, ASK

"Why won't you let me love you?"

This is the exasperated cry of not knowing how to get access into the other's heart. We were created as much to love as to be loved. When we're not allowed, it can crush our sense of worth. This quote could be heard from anyone, but maybe especially from a wife or husband.

Sometimes the reason we're not let in is because we've not been trustworthy. If you violate confidences publicly, or emotionally manipulate, then you'll eventually be less trusted. And no matter how much love you have to give them, the degree to which your spouse trusts you is the degree to which they will let you love them.

Sometimes, we're not let in because of the other's fear to trust. We may be fully trustworthy, but they may have been wounded by betrayal and lack of commitment.

It's brave and frightening to ask the other where we violated their trust. But they're longing for you to ask, because they desperately want to be loved.

1 Corinthians 13:7

THANKSGIVING

Embedded in the overwhelming promises of Ephesians 1 is a game-changing revelation. Ready? When God thinks about what He's thankful for . . . *it's us!*

Paul asks for our hearts to be enlightened so we'll know the hope of God's calling and "the riches of the glory of His inheritance in the saints." God's riches that He has inherited through all that His Son has done is *us,* the saints! That's mind-boggling. Paul's asking that the light of our hearts would burst on, partly so we would see God giving thanks for us!

We are overwhelmed in thankfulness for His thankfulness of us.

After all we've gotten ourselves into, the God of the universe counts us as His treasure. This week, this Thanksgiving, it would be a magnificent reflection to let that thought wash over you: God is thankful for you!

Ephesians 1:18

I NEED A COUNSELOR?

Living in relationships of trust can significantly assist in resolving your compulsive sin issues. Sometimes, not so much. The "relational spaghetti" and addiction patterns can carry too much concealed insight and history.

At this point, you may want to challenge the assumption that your own stab at self-cure will hold. Because your answers worked for a season, you may now resist, even in the face of repeated setbacks, a counselor. Yet, you also recognize you're clearly stuck in the same patterns that gripped you before you "solved" your issues. You may assume that you simply didn't try hard enough. But we think you probably did try hard enough.

One of the most mature things you might do now is to engage a therapist. Many of us on the Trueface team have done so, and we've benefitted enormously. We're not in favor of therapists who cannot apply the gospel of grace to your experience, but we are all for trained, seasoned, and biblically anchored therapists. You, or a friend, may be ready for such.

Romans 15:13-14

WHEN BABY ELEPHANTS GROW

The risk with a small elephant in the room is that many who might call out a large elephant can somehow stomach a smaller one.

Perhaps the little elephant is you; maybe it is relational hubris in your life, which you think others should see as reasonable. Or it could be some passive-aggressive character who keeps damaging your organizational culture. The risky illusion that an "unimportant" issue can be ignored often morphs into community disillusionment. Over time, little elephants tend to consume more people and grow into complicated demoralizing creatures.

Dietrich Bonhoeffer imagined what happens to community when we casually let little elephants become sizable problem mammals: "Just as surely as God desires to lead us to a knowledge of genuine Christian fellowship, so surely we must be overwhelmed by a great disillusionment with others, with Christians in general, and, if we are fortunate, with ourselves. By sheer grace, God will not permit us to live even for a brief period in a dream world."

Beware the baby elephant. In grace, you'll become healthier for it.

1 Corinthians 4:4

WHAT IF YOU MADE THIS ALL UP?

"What if I made this all up in my head?" If you haven't thought this yet, you probably will one day. It's scary to suddenly be confronted with shocking doubt of what you were convinced you believed so entirely.

Don't panic. Next time the thought shows up, you can respond, "First, I know me. I'm not capable of making up a Person so wonderful. So there's that. Second, I've never run into anyone able to make up anyone nearly as magnificent as Jesus. He's an entirely different category from all myths, fables, legends, or gods. So there's that."

It's cool you're willing to risk everything on Him. If He doesn't turn out to exist, then eternity is highly overrated anyway! You'll take your chances that such goodness was not just in your head. If you could miss heaven by believing in Jesus, then the creator of such a place is too evil to comprehend. So there's that. Take that, doubt!

James 1:6

DECEMBER

"Deep inside each soul, God
sows a seed of destiny."

-The Ascent of a Leader

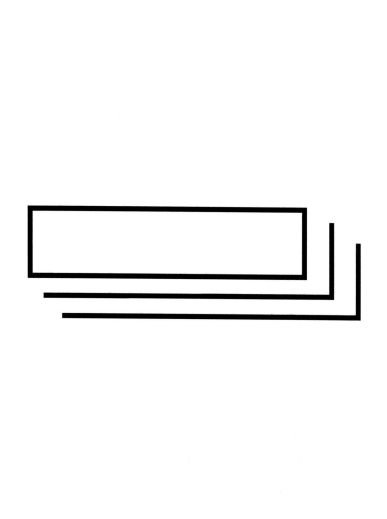

HIGHLY SUCCESSFUL PEOPLE

Perhaps you've seen commercials or read books that tell you what "highly successful" people do. It can feel intimidating and create a bunch of angst. Because, for crying out loud, you want to be successful!

Perhaps some successful people do some similar things some of the time. But what is a successful person anyway? You probably can think of some folk you'd like to emulate who don't take testosterone cream or use a certain time-management system.

Those who trust Jesus and others with themselves are the successful. At least Proverbs thinks so. To have your paths directed fully by God. Wow! That sounds pretty successful, doesn't it? Can the testosterone cream promise that?

Such folk may not make the most money or attract the opposite sex as promised on the late-night infomercials. But don't be intimidated. God directing your path gets you about everywhere you need to go. He may cause you to experience some incredible life lessons. Just give yourself permission to discern what success you are looking for.

Proverbs 3:5-6

A TSUNAMI OF CALAMITY

Today may be one of those days. You can feel it, complete with ominous background music. Things are building for a really, really bad day. You've been here before. You can't stop it. You can't fight against it. It would be comical if it wasn't so destructive. It feels like a tsunami of complications, delays, appliances breaking, dash lights appearing, and relationships straining. And for some reason, God is allowing it all to happen.

Your mission today, should you choose to accept it, is to simply stay in the arena. You don't have to advance the Kingdom or prove anything. Just endure.

But when you get Home, you may discover this was one of your finest days. Darkness was trying to unravel you, and instead you trusted Jesus and didn't take the bait.

Nothing is random. God's in control. Evil won't win. Everything can be eventually mopped up. Take in a movie. Hug those you love and say, "Today I'm just trying to duck. Did I mention I love you and I'm all in?"

1 Peter 5:8-11

TAPPING INTO THE WISE

Who's the wisest person you know? Maybe think of several. Wise people can give sound application to truth in the chaotic, confusing daily events of life. They seem to see life in overarching principles. They've put all their eggs in the basket of God and His grace. Their lives pulse with a sense of settledness. The word "peace" comes to mind.

It would bless that person tremendously to tell him or her how you see them. Remember, affirmation does not puff up but humbles. It would be astute of you to set up a time to sit with that person. Set aside several hours, maybe to ask only this simple question: "How do you practically acquire wisdom?"

Once they're convinced you really want to know, they'll go on for quite a while without stopping. You may decide you'd like to ask that person to sit again and talk of such things as part of your friendship.

Now look who's getting all wise!

Proverbs 22:17-19

RETELLING THE WONDROUS

If you don't tell someone about moments that are magnificent or astonishingly and surprisingly good, you'll regret it later. It's easy to take magical moments for granted, as though they'll come again. You shouldn't. You come by this way once.

Telling someone about the wondrous does so many good things. It shows the other that they matter to you. You're offering them the gift of your passion and heart. Telling about your experience captures what the event did to you, evocatively, in a way no picture or video can. It also encourages your closest friends and family that they don't get to hear just the hard stuff about you but also your joy.

Maybe most important, you're giving glory to God, for all these events are from His hand. Your message to those around you is that this life counts. The delight in how you tell it allows them maybe to give glory to God—or at least to consider such a God might exist.

Psalm 40

DRESS REHEARSALS

Maybe you're in the doldrums, where you can't find much immediate significance in what you're doing. Maybe you're living in pajamas, not leaving the house for days at a time, herding infants. Or you're training for a new career, away from family, in a cold, dank city, eating take-out off a hotel bedspread.

You believe it's ultimately important. But day by day? That's another story.

Yet such mundane time is vital! You get to wrestle with big concepts and ask big questions without big consequences. You can imagine key life scenes before they arrive. You are rehearsing the power of Christ in you. So later, when the hard choices emerge, the chaos of the moment won't knock you off center. Practicing trust gives you poise under pressure.

In some free moments, think ahead to some hard scenarios and imagine how your new nature would want to respond. When the scenario one day does arrive, you'll be able to say, "Well, well, well. Big issue, I've seen you coming! God, here we go!"

Luke 1:78-79

OUR DEAR GOD

How are we to be honest with You about ourselves and not hide from You? It feels so incredibly vulnerable for You to know all the worst about us yet convince ourselves to believe You love us as much as anyone in the universe. It doesn't make sense.

Maybe it's why we perform and put on a facade that we're better, healthier, or purer than we are in this moment. It's the silliest and most outlandish lie we tell ourselves—that if we bluff maybe You'll fall for it. It sounds stupid even saying that. But there it is. Maybe we doubt Your shed blood is enough to keep us perfectly clean before You. Saying that sounds more simpleminded than the last stupid thing. But there it is.

We're tired of all the stupid. Your Word says Your blood is powerful enough to keep us endlessly in Your wondrous delight. We're going to risk that it's true. We may question Your taste, but we're tired of mistrusting Your ability.

1 Peter 1:17-19

BRAVE ANSWERS

We watch a YouTube clip of someone saving a child from a frozen river. We are awed by their brave decision. And we wonder if we could do the same.

Bravery is not only a choice decided in a moment. It is more an action formed by answers to excellent questions asked along the way.

"Why am I here?" "What do I value?" "How do those I admire live?" "What would I risk my life for?" "Is there something beyond this life if I put it at risk?" "How do I love another?"

You can't always tell when you've decided your answer to those questions. You can't predict where you will have that decision revealed.

Technique doesn't always work in a split-second decision. But love does.

Sometimes bravery looks like not shaming your son when he shows you a speeding ticket. Other times it looks like standing up for a new kid being berated in a high school locker room.

Ask your questions. Trust God with your answers. Be brave.

John 15:13; Joshua 1:9

HYPERSENSITIVITY

There comes a time when you can no longer self-defend, blame others, or justify your overreactions. Apparently, some of what others are pointing out is largely about you. When you imagine that you are being continually over-critiqued, under-appreciated, or regularly slighted, it can create an exaggerated reaction that can confuse and repel those you love, work with, or try to teach.

Hypersensitivity results from some kind of wounding or deception. Sometimes it's traceable. Often it's not. The antidote, though, is unerringly traceable. It will not necessarily eliminate your overreactions instantly. But once you embrace it, you will see yourself more honestly. It's this: You are not your wounding. Jesus died to free you from that and any lesser identity. You can now let God and others help describe you to you, a beloved, changed, and emerging Christ-defined you. You can let the slights come and allow the unreasonable critiques to continue. He is healing the wounding, and you are increasingly reflecting Christ in you.

Romans 12:3

THE MIDDLE OF THE NIGHT

It's dark-thirty and you've got that fear feeling. The feeling often revolves around money, retirement, or the thought you might live your last years in a shipping crate along a freeway underpass.

If you're younger, it may involve panic about those thesis papers due next week, or the odd conversation yesterday with your boyfriend. "We're breaking up for sure," you reason. "He's attracted to that girl in English Lit with the expensive shoes. I'd be cuter too if my dad was paying for college." And on and on.

Before you spin completely out of control, remember this about those middle-of-the-night exaggerations. In the morning, your life will still be there, but without the exaggerations. You could simply call out, "Jesus, help me. I'm overwhelmed." That prayer is more than sufficient. His name takes the power from darkness. Try to go back to sleep; but if you can't, why not get a head start on that Lit paper? Whatever you choose, good night.

Philippians 4:6-7

CALLING FOULS ON YOURSELF

Few things break up the rhythm of a pick-up basketball game like players who refuse to call fouls on themselves. The game is built on this unspoken honor, that each player will call their own name if they've fouled another. It makes the game run smoothly and everyone gets along well.

When we begin to learn grace, God teaches us to tell on ourselves. We tell our faults and previously hidden behaviors to God and others. We are surprised to discover that we're able to be loved more. Friends don't run away but usually draw closer. Vulnerability somehow engenders affection. It's how friends become indispensable to each other. We are not competing against each other but playing for each other, which makes our honesty life-giving and essential.

So, when you have told on yourself, who has drawn closer? It would be essential to tell them what that's meant to you, to thank them for making it safer to call fouls on yourself. It's a delightfully important pick-up game to be part of.

James 5:16

A WRAPPED BISCOTTI

Those who love get to meet needs. Attention can be a fun need to meet. For example, friends, spouses, parents and children can select an object, maybe like a wrapped biscotti that some of the airlines give out like confetti. You hide it in a place they may not notice for a day or two. When they do find it, usually it makes them smile. "I was thought about. I'm known. I'm not alone." After a hard day, with relationship struggles at work, that little biscotti, or something like it, can offer a meaningful gift of attention.

Then love gets reciprocated. The other delights in getting to hide it in a place that you both uniquely would know about. The more creative the hiding place, the more fun and the more of a sense of being particularly known.

Love is sometimes exceedingly fun.

John 15:10-11

AN INTEGRITY FOR THEIR BENEFIT

A moralistic culture feels palpably different from a culture of grace. In the first, we are taught to develop our character in isolation and then maintain it in public. In the second, we discover that character is formed in community and then tested out in isolation.

This fundamental shift of how we approach our maturity can seriously undermine the hypocrisy we're accused of. The first conviction often assumes a superior behavior from a superior time alone with God. The second displays an authenticity in front of others, from believing we mature best when we trust God and others with who we really are. We are learning to believe who God says we are: righteous, holy, without condemnation, and full of His ongoing favor and delight, which helps us truthfully confront and process with others our character shortcomings.

Your integrity is not a badge to wear for *your* benefit, but a way for others to trust and access your influence for *their* benefit.

Whew, what a relief. Wow, what a purpose.

2 Corinthians 3:3

ACCOUNTABILITY AND PROTECTION

If we're going to allow others access to our lives, then it shouldn't make us more hidden than before. This is the catch with the most popular method of dealing with sin. *Accountability* works best for task. *Protection* is best for person. With sin, accountability becomes an expression of law, causing you to resent and hide from those closest to you. "Hey, you promised to tell me!" We were too embarrassed. Now we're shamefully embarrassed. We'll hide better next time.

Protection gives opportunity to hide nothing, because it's anchored in trust. The protector stands beside you, with your sin in front of you both, not between. The protector earns trust so that in the moment of greatest temptation, you might be willing to tell them the sin you're *intending* to commit. The battle moves from your superior will-power to trust. This is grace: to believe that you won't be thrown under the bus. Instead, you'll be loved more in such risk and vulnerability. In this way, God employs the trust of real friendships, robbing sin of its power. That's protection.

James 5:19-20

HEAVEN HERE AND NOW

There are days, many days, when no answers or encouraging word in the here and now will do. This planet will never have enough comfort. No amount of resources or good fortune can override that. You might not readily want to believe this is true. Don't blame yourself. There's a reason some have called this world the "vale of tears."

But Peter writes that you've obtained "an inheritance which is imperishable and undefiled and will not fade away, reserved in heaven for you." It cannot be destroyed, it can never spoil, and it will not lose its value. Your name's on it, awaiting you in heaven! Peter says this causes us to fully rejoice when we embrace it.

Our lives on earth last about nine minutes and heaven is, well, f-o-r-e-v-e-r! Our true home isn't this small, guarded, self-protective world you currently see, but a Home you've not yet even dared to imagine. Try that on the next day your world feels broken. Like today perhaps.

1 Peter 1:3-6

IRREDUCIBLE VERSES

Some of us still carry a propensity to feel condemned by scripture. Maybe this will help. God has given us the amazingly wonderful gift of "irreducible verses," passages that cannot be altered by anything we do.

In addition, nothing God will ever do can change their meaning, such as, Romans 8:1: "Therefore, there is no condemnation for those who are in Christ Jesus." None. Nada. Zip. Zilch. No condemnation. That washes over a whole lot of confusing verses.

John 15:9 says, "Just as the Father has loved me, I have also loved you." There is no greater love than the Father's love for the Son. Jesus says His love for you is of the exact same measure—unchangeable, unable to be reduced.

Galatians 2:20 says, "I have been crucified with Christ and it is no longer I who live, but Christ lives in me." Totally and completely transformed. A new creature.

In only these three verses, almost every condemnation challenge in scripture is met. There are dozens more. Meditate on that goodness.

Galatians 2:20

WHEN GRACE GOT CHALLENGED (PART ONE)

For much of your faith life, you strived so hard to know that you'd done enough. It never quite got you there. You never felt the full acceptance and delight of God. You studied, sang the songs, and prayed with all your heart. But it wasn't enough.

Then came the message of grace. It was there all along, but suddenly you dared to believe there was no other shoe about to drop. It felt too good to be true. It began to reframe how you saw God, yourself, and every moment of life. No condemnation. No pretending. Only the full-on love of Jesus.

Then along came a visiting preacher teaching on some scary-sounding verses. They seemed to yell that grace was not enough. There was something more you must do. And God was so disappointed with you. It knocked you for a loop.

Fear not. It all had to be tested. You can't make this grace hold. Jesus did that several thousand years ago. It's good news. No person can change that.

Hebrews 13:8-9

WHEN GRACE GOT CHALLENGED (PART TWO)

So this grace you never thought you'd find, and then did . . . feels lost again.

It was almost better before you knew it existed. At least you knew where you stood. Now you feel the worst kind of alone. Were all those who believed in grace duped and you're the only one who has realized it was all just a fairy tale?

Gird your loins, friend. You've been challenged to put your full weight upon the gospel. Either Jesus has accomplished your full righteousness or this whole deal is a carnival barker's lie. *The miraculous always feels too good to be true*. But if you're duped, you're at least with Paul: ". . . so that I may gain Christ, and may be found in Him, not having a righteousness of my own derived from the Law, but that which is through faith in Christ, the righteousness which comes from God on the basis of faith."

You're not alone. Now get back to living. We need you.

Hebrews 4:16

CONVERSATIONS JESUS MIGHT HAVE HAD

(With Nicodemus, early in the evening, somewhere in Jerusalem)

Nicodemus: "Rabbi, we know you are from God. But, and I'm just being honest here, you get to wear sandals and a comfortable robe. Look at me. I'm dressed up like this all the time. Is it fair to bring that up?"

Jesus: "Yes, it does get hot here in the summer months."

Nicodemus: "I'd be lying if I didn't say I perspire under these layers."

Jesus: "Nicodemus, some day, long from now, when your name is not as popular with parents, I will cause mankind to produce a 'wicking' fabric. It will literally remove the perspiration. Rather miraculous, if I say so."

Nicodemus: "What a time to be alive! What could be wrong with introducing this wicking now?"

Jesus: "Don't even get me started. Now, tell me, what really brings you here this evening?"

This is the last time the matter was spoken of. But every now and then when they would see each other on a warm day, the two would nod knowingly to each other.

John 3:1-21

DEATH AND GRIEF

Maybe you've recently lost someone important to you.

Maybe you've already noticed there's no definable beginning, middle, or closure. It's mostly just hills and valleys of grey grief. There's pain. Then dull sorrow. Then moments of clear insight and memory. Then sharp new pain, more confusion, doubt. God doesn't fix it or stop it the way you hoped. He knows this journey. He's lived it. He won't easily block what is your privilege to face.

He's right here with you. God loved that important someone more than anyone, ever. God's been grieving too, but now mostly for you. Yes, you'll see them again in the land where all this discordant, life-sapping grief will melt away into ecstatic reunion. But not yet. For now you're here, in the valley of the shadow.

God is right beside you. You will need close friends too. Your hope is evidenced by the way you live in the valley until then.

1 Corinthians 15:55-57

TO CHANGE THE WORLD

God made you to change the world. He made you for influence. One way you can express this influence is through money. The Bible talks a lot about it. But we don't.

Even with close friends, we freeze up around money talk. Money is funny.

But what if you did talk about it? What would it look like? Well, it would start with the truth that God gave us a new heart.

And the good news is that this new identity is generous. This new heart is bountiful, unselfish, kindhearted, charitable, full of brotherly love, openhanded, and compassionate. This is who we are in Christ.

So next time you freeze up around money talk, rejoice that your new identity is actually generous. This means that you can talk about generosity and even your fears. You can ask questions such as, "What do you give to and why?" You can ask them at church. Ask them over dinner with your family. This is risky and well worth it.

Matthew 6:21

IMMANUEL
(PART ONE)

He was given a name to explain Him exactly. *Immanuel*. "God with us."

He is not a theology or a religion. He is not an icon, or a mythical movement leader. He is not an allegory, an ideal, or a way of life. He is not a memory. He is not a faint echo from a far-off land. He is not just the stuff of stories. He is not less real now than to those who could touch Him. He does not belong to any denomination. He is not a bedtime story created to make children shape up. He is not just on special occasions. He is not only in the miracle. He is not here because you called hard enough or because you earned it.

He is not a metaphor. He's not here in a riddle or a formula. He is not here by wishing He was real.

He is God with us.

Matthew 1:18-25

IMMANUEL
(PART TWO)

He is here. Right now. Fully, completely. He is in you, around you, with you, over you, about you, for you, on time, in the middle of, surrounding you and the ones you love.

In complete power, He is communicating as clearly as at any time in history, doing perfectly to you, for you, by you, thinking about you every moment, walking directly into the middle of your worst fear, your pain, your loneliness, your doubts, your insecurity, your sickness, your tragedy, your fragility, your hope, your joy, your peace, your dreams, your relationships, your love, your longing to have your life count.

He is here. He is champion and author of every beauty you find yourself longing for. He is the one who stands over you in the darkest hour. He is lifting you up when you are too exhausted, too devastated, too hopeless, too failed, too compromised, too far gone. He has not forgotten. He is no less able now than back then. He is not beyond where your prayers reach.

He is God with us.

Luke 1:26-38

12.22

IMMANUEL (PART THREE)

He is in this terrible and beautiful season. The holidays. He's rushing around with you in malls trying to find gifts. He's with you when the carols make you sad, thinking of the Christmases you can't bring back.

He's with you in every memory, every hope, with intimacy stronger than words. He is drawing you to the cross in this very moment, the heart of Christmas, to pause in awe of His endless love. He is here to protect you from despair, the condemning voices, the regrets. He is here when you think that everyone might truly be better off without you around. He is here to whisper who you are. He is here to bundle up and walk beneath December's sky with you, hands in pockets, smiling, with all the time in the world. He is here to declare your worth. He is here to be glorified, enjoyed, trusted, and worshiped by you. He'd love to drive around and look at the lights with you.

He is God with us.

Luke 1:39-56

IMMANUEL (PART FOUR)

He is here whether you want Him here or not. He's here in all power, doing exactly the right thing, even when you don't believe it. He is here in the pain you never thought He'd allow. He is here in the yelling at Him you thought you'd never dare. He's here completely for you in this moment. He is God with us, God with them, God with the wicked and twisted, all at once. He is unafraid to be present in a world that questions His decisions, why He doesn't do more, why He doesn't stop it all. He is here and does not deflect our accusations. He is here in our arrogance imagining that we care more than He does. He is perfect love. He is my new name: Christ in me! He is Immanuel.

He is not here the way we demand. He is here exactly in the way we need. Beyond cliches or sentiment, He is the gift. His name says it all. God with us.

Merry Christmas.

Luke 2:1-20

WHEN NEW STAYED NEW

Christmas Day. For many of us as kids, it was the day each year when the world became new. We unwrapped toys while we ate more cinnamon rolls and bacon than our little bodies should rightly hold. Magic. Magic with a stomachache perhaps, but magic.

Christmas Day exposed what we longed for but couldn't articulate. *We* wanted to be new—and not for a day or a month. We wanted joy, hope, and goodness, and to celebrate it with a cinnamon roll. We wanted a new that wouldn't end.

But that is the very thing we were celebrating. Such a day had already come. At the Resurrection, the day Jesus rose from the grave, life *did* become new! New life, new power, limitless love. Freedom from sin, freedom from lies and hiding. The moment we put our faith in Jesus, we knew this was what we'd been waiting for all along. Jesus made new stay new.

The Merriest of Christmases to you from the Trueface team!

Revelation 21:5-7

EVERYONE LOVES STORIES

Once upon a time. Those four words just might be some of the most powerful in the world. Regardless of whether you're five or sixty-five, live in Duluth or Damascus, and change your oil regularly or let's just say irregularly, simply hearing "once upon a time" makes us all pause and lean in to pay attention to what comes next. Because what always follows is a story.

The undisputed greatest storyteller ever? Jesus. He knew we all carry this innate love for stories, so that's what He consistently used to communicate His good news of grace. "There was a sower who went out to sow . . ." "There was a man who had two sons . . ." and on and on. Mark's Gospel indicates that Jesus was never without a story for the people.

That's wise to remember as we desire to share with others God's message of freedom and grace. Many in our world are weary of sermons. That's fair. But a story? They're practically impossible to resist.

Mark 4:26-34

THE RIGHTNESS
OF GOD

The single most-important experience any believer can have is finding yourself believing, then doubting, and then resting in the absolute goodness and perfect rightness of God.

Maybe especially in the events you least understand. The ones that leave you scratching your head.

All your efforts to pass judgment upon His ways will not gain you what you most need.

Once you're relatively convinced that you've put your hope in the true God, then, as the poets and songwriters have long said, "It's a matter of trust."

So go play horseshoes, or treat a friend to a milkshake. The confusing firestorm will go on for a while just fine without you. God has this. If not, then we're all up the proverbial creek without the conventional means of locomotion.

Revelation 15:1-4

A BENEVOLENT RULER

A beautiful aspect of grace is that it releases us to give instead of take. When we remain unsure about our identity, still trying to prove who we are, we inevitably turn inward. We become takers.

Grace turns us into givers. One way this can play out in our lives is in how we interact with the natural environment. God's stunning, explosively creative creation has been given to us to rule. When we are living as takers, as orphans who need to prove they have a home, we can become harsh, exacting rulers. We dominate. We take.

But when we know we are secure, delighted-in heirs to a glorious kingdom, we get to become benevolent, generous rulers. No longer tyrants, we can cultivate, raise up, and tenderly care for what's been given to us. We get to look after the earth as tenderly as God looks after us. Today, ask God to show you one way you can become a more gracious caretaker of His creation.

Genesis 1:28

PATIENCE AND DIGNITY

We are not strangers to working on our life issues. Many of us have spent countless hours trying to improve certain behaviors—it may even be working to an extent. But for those in Christ, there is so much more than human discipline at play.

How about patience? Sure, you can choose to not say snarky things standing in a line that is making you late. But are you still boiling inside? Is that patience? Well then, let's not work on patience. Let's remember what we already believe about a different concept: dignity.

Every person in this line—even the one causing this delay—has profound dignity. Far more dignity than they experience each day. The more God convinces you of His delight in you and your dignity, the less you will miss it in others

And the more we see the dignity in others, the more easily we can express the patience God has already placed in us. Seems strange, doesn't it? Well, that sounds a lot like God.

Psalm 8:4-9

THE LEADER IN YOU

No matter your age, culture, or status, you are affected by leaders. Many of these you know. Some, who impact your daily life—such as government leaders—you may never meet. Yet, all of these leaders have something in common. They will influence even more out of who they are than what they do.

So, when you think about leaders, remember the priority of leader development over leadership development. The first deals with character. The second involves competencies. Both are crucial, but only the first can protect and leverage the second. When the Bible sets criteria for leaders, it focuses on the first. Unfortunately, most cultures invest far more resources on leadership development than on leader development, ironically leaving both at risk.

In its broader meaning, a leader is any person of influence. This means there is a leader in you. No matter your age, culture, or status, you affect others, including other leaders. As you influence, center on the "first things" and God will integrate your character and competencies for the great benefit of others.

1 Timothy 3:1-7

REMEMBERING JESUS

When Jesus asked His band to "remember Him" using the bread and wine as simple symbols, they weren't in an elegant setting. There was little liturgical order to things, just eating, talking, washing feet, praying. Jesus didn't say how frequently to take up those symbols nor that this should always occur in a church setting. He simply said, "as *often* as you do this . . ."

You can remember the unfathomable riches of Christ's grace by taking bread and juice with you to all kinds of places for all kinds of reasons.

Communion means "the sharing or exchanging of intimate thoughts and feelings." Commune with Jesus, on your own or with friends. Every week or every day. On mountaintops or at the beach. In your home or in your car. When you receive a promotion or lose a job . . . or a loved one. When graduating from school or receiving a gift. You are remembering that no gift will ever match Jesus in your life. He will enjoy this time and so will you.

2 Corinthians 8:9

ACKNOWLEDGMENTS

From the very start we decided to produce this as a team—a Trueface devotional. From conception, writing and editing content, to choosing covers and titles, it has been an exercise in trying out what we've been teaching and modeling to others. We've tried to submit to each others' strengths and protect each others' weaknesses.

Instead of creating a hodgepodge of random entries (like a neighborhood talent show), it has brought out the best of who we are, individually and collectively. In some ways our entire staff at Trueface (see them at trueface.org) has contributed to this book. Because we're all friends and carriers of trusting our identities in Christ, this has not been a changing of the guard but a learning that all of us bring talents, new ideas, new directions, and mad skills, which would be missed if we kept just doing things the same. Including these voices has brought a freshness and nuance to the message, folding in the experiences of different generations.

Trusted other friends were employed in their strengths as well. Our "resident theologian," Stewart Black, is back again. He has helped us match applicable, relevant verses and passages with each devotional. John Blase is a remarkably thoughtful and skilled editor. Perhaps most needed on this particular book was his ability to condense sentences and paragraphs into concise and winsome clarity. We really enjoy doing projects with him. Steen Hudson added his passion and enthusiasm for biblical generosity and also contributed one of the devotionals.

Newtype has vitally improved the way we tell our story through publishing. Their value to us is profound, in their expertise, commitment to excellence, and grammatical editing. They worked tirelessly with our team to achieve exactly what we wanted in every detail.

As always, none of this gets to happen without the leadership, direction and love of our Trueface Board. This is not only a governing board but also a group of friends who stand together in the best and hardest events of life. They trust God deeply and protect our families well.

We owe much gratitude to the dean, Karen Hunt, and faculty of our High Trust Leader Course. They have taught us much about what it means to trust for today. We thank our Trueface Advisory Council, our organizational partners, and those who have given their prayers. Scores of people have generously offered their financial gifts to this nonprofit ministry. They have freed up our team to bring programs and projects of insight and delight—like this book—to many around the world, and the proceeds from this book will be reinvested alongside these generous gifts to bring the freedom of the gospel of grace to hundreds of thousands.

Finally, this book is for you—hopefully, more or less directly from Him. It is about God, for God, to God, from God, and about seeing life together with God. We may have missed His intentions on more than one entry, but we've tried to best imagine what He wants to say to each one of us. It is the reason we wrote this book. Thanks for giving us the privilege all these years.

The Trueface Team

INDEX

CONTINUATION OF COPYRIGHT PAGE AND RESOURCES

April, "Sharing Jesus In A Post-Christian Age": Bruce Cockburn. "Lovers in a Dangerous Time." *Stealing Fire* True North, Gold Mountain, A&M, 1984.

May, "Destiny": *The Trail: A Tale About Discovering God's Will* by Ed Underwood Copyright © 2014 by Ed Underwood. Tyndale House Publishers, Inc.

June: *Lay It Down: Living in the Freedom of the Gospel* by Bill Tell Copyright © 2015 by Bill Tell. A NavPress resource published in alliance with Tyndale House Publishers, Inc.

July, "A Gentle Person": *Bread for the Journey, A Daybook of Wisdom and Faith* by Henri Nouwen Copyright © 1997 by Henri J. M. Nouwen. Used by permission of HarperCollins.

September, "Safe Not Soft": *The Discipline of Disturbance: Stop Waiting for Life to be Easy* by Hud McWilliams Copyright © 2018 by Hud McWilliams. Equip Press.

September, "The Dance of Doubt and Faith": *Wishful Thinking: A Theological ABC* by Frederick Buechner Copyright © 1973 by Frederick Buechner. HarperCollins.

October: *The Kingdom Life* by Willard, Thrall, McNicol, Matthews, Hull, Meyer, Reynoso, Fuller, Demarest, Glerup, Averbeck Morton Copyright © by The Navigators. NavPress.

November, "Secrets": Jacob, J. Pamer, J. (Producers), & Esau, E. (Director). (2017). *The Heart of Man* [Motion Picture]. USA: Sypher Studios.

November, "Christianity And Politics": Taken from *What's So Amazing About Grace?* by Philip Yancey Copyright © 1997 by Philip D. Yancey. Use by permission of Zondervan. Gratis Use: Text